And How My Spirit Soars

*Learning to Pack for
an Extraordinary Journey*

And How
My Spirit Soars

Learning to Pack for
an Extraordinary Journey

SHARON SIMPSON JOSEPH

SpiritSoars
INCORPORATED

Atlanta

Published by Spirit Soars, Inc.
4840 Roswell Road, B-100
Atlanta, GA 30342
877-434-SOAR
www.spiritsoars.com • journey@spiritsoars.com

This work is autobiographical in nature. Some of the names have been changed and some characters fictionalized.

Cover and book design: Jill Dible
Cover painting "Rejoice": Monica Stewart
Editorial: Drollene P. Brown and Jill Mason

Library of Congress Control Number: 2001096270
First Edition
ISBN 0-9678543-3-4
Printed in the United States of America on acid-free paper.

10   9   8   7   6   5   4   3   2   1

Dedication

Long before Julia came into my womb, the title *And How My Spirit Soars* was born. How was I to know that our baby Julia was the soaring spirit I so lovingly nurtured all those years? My husband, Robert, and I spoke of two births, *Soars* and Julia. How was I to know that in fact they are one?

Soars is dedicated
to
Julia
our soaring spirit.

"*As babies, I believe we can fly.*
It comes naturally to us, like drinking mother's milk and smiling into the sky.
We take flights of abandon and exploration. We learn much about the world and what we are to do here.
Our journeys.
Then, we begin to walk. Things start to slow down. Make less sense.
And we can spend much of our time here on earth searching to capture the magic and euphoria of those early voyages. When flights of fancy were a natural part of our existence. And walking an anomaly."
(*Sharon, September 1999*)

Not so for our daughter Julia. She never had to slow down and search for the magic. Or wonder about her mission and existence. She knew why she was here. Her journey of nine months began and ended in the womb. And though she did not survive her birth—she taught me to fly.

And all of us—how to let our spirits soar.

Sharon, May 2001

Contents

Introduction

YESTERDAY I FOUND MY VOICE

Yesterday
I found my voice
Today I live to tell about it
I didn't shout from the rooftops
Didn't whisper or scream
But I spoke, and the words that I heard
Were my own

Yesterday I found my voice
Today I live to tell about it
And I sing a hallelujah chorus
In a key I've never tried before
Tell about it. Tell about it

I am a warrior woman
I won't roll over or die
Give up, dry up
Or be sucked up

Yesterday I found my voice
And it's here to stay
Cause I can't let it go
I chant over and over
Write on all my pages
Say it again and again in my head
And then I open my mouth and cry out loud

Yesterday I found my voice
Today I'm here to shout about it
And this one's for you
All those who know exactly what
I'm talking about. . . .

Love,
Sharon

I like that poem. Every time I read the words, it makes me feel like I did when I wrote it. Yesterday, I found my voice. Today, I live to tell about it.

Somewhere I heard that the most powerful segment of opportunity we experience regularly is each new day. I've come to celebrate that message.

My journals are an affirmation of this belief for me. I've been writing journals since I was a child, sometimes in the craziest of places or situations. I'm glad I kept them. Because this is a unique chance to share them with you . . . to tell a story as it happened . . . and to pass on my discoveries.

If I had wanted you to simply understand me, I'd have written an autobiography that spells out plainly who I am and what I think of the world—told of course, in the midst of clever metaphors, intriguing testimonies and symbolic and meaningful narrative. So maybe this isn't so much about me as it is about desiring to share something with you, wanting to express feelings, explorations, and consciousness . . . to strike a familiar chord within you, or perhaps a whisper of emotion, but certainly to sense, to touch, to know.

The intimate stories I share with you are based upon those journals, and in the earlier years, taken from memory, to transport you on this journey. Through these adventures, sometimes amazing, embarrassing, triumphant, achingly painful, uplifting, wild or funny, I have come to realize that what I pack for each stage of the journey can make the difference between a course of abundance and one of limitation.

What are the precious essentials to pack? What is the baggage to leave behind?

I invite you now to take this journey . . . whether it encourages your dreams, awakens healing to make peace with an experience of your own, shines a light for your voyage of constant opportunity and growth, or makes you laugh out loud.

Perhaps we wrestle with some of the same life questions to which you, too, are seeking answers. I hope you find my challenges and hard-won lessons exhilarating and helpful.

And that you'll feel you've made a friend.

Yesterday I found my voice. Today I'm here to shout about it. *And How My Spirit Soars* is my gift offering.

Recipe For Bouk-a-Shouk

*They say that it is the early years of our lives
that form the foundation for who we are
and how we begin life's journey.
It's like an Awakening,
learning what is inside ourselves,
and what's outside, in the world . . .*

Our Bouk-a-Shouk Recipe:

Three crayon filings from your favorite color Crayolas

(sky blue or rose are best!)

One part dreams from the night before

Three strong squeezes of Crest toothpaste

(Pre-heat Easy Bake Oven)

Laugh and gather four colored pencils (shave and add to mixture)

Add a secret and a hug

Johnson's Baby Powder for texture and great smell

Next stir in favorite lotion

Must be pink!

Pour in Easy Bake pan

Bake for two minutes under hot light bulb

Smile, slice and eat.

Feeds two special, imaginative young sisters

P.S. Tastes best when served in our bedroom in Rochdale.

With love always,
Your sister, Sherry
May 1999

September 5, 1966
Queens, New York • The van is big and fast, taking me farther and farther away from home. There are no other children in here. Only me so far. I am the first stop.

I can't see the bus driver behind his chair. I am trying to be a big girl. But inside I don't feel so big. Look at my feet. They stick out off the seat. I have on my blue corduroy jumper that Mommy loves me to wear. It is a special day.

My first day of school.

In my head, I say again, slowly, In-ter-na-tion-al Day School, that's what Mommy says it's called.

I miss my sister. She is too young for school. I picture Sherry and me at home making bouk-a-shouk. The recipe only works when it's the two of us. You can't make it alone.

Wait, I hear music. What is it? If I listen really hard I can hear it! It is playing on the bus driver's radio. *"Hey there, Georgie Girl. . . . swinging down the street so fancy free . . ."* I know that song. I even know most of the words. I sing it, very quiet. I practice so that even if another little boy or girl sits next to me, they can't hear me sing. Push my back hard up against the seat and sit up straighter. I'll just sit here and sing and think only of the song and not about being scared. I look straight out the window where I can see the road ahead and sing "Georgie Girl."

May 5, 1967 • People say I am shy. I guess that's because I don't say much when I meet new kids. Or when we see Mommy's friends at the store, I hide behind her leg. And when we go to Grandmother and Grandpop Simpsons', me and Sherry are the youngest cousins, and even though Sherry's not shy, neither of us talks much there either.

What is shy? I think it must be a bad thing because Mommy seems worried about it. I heard Mommy telling Daddy that she hopes nursery school will help. She said I didn't used to be shy when I was a really little kid. I was always clapping my hands and smiling at people . . . that I was just born happy.

I don't know why I am shy. Does that mean there is something wrong with me?

November 14, 1967 • My teacher, Miss Pearl, holds the book close to her face. When she stops reading to ask us a question, she turns the book around so that we can see the pictures. She sits in a large wooden chair, a huge version of the tiny chairs we have.

"Why did Horatio the tiger lose his stripes?" Miss Pearl asks us.

I think about Horatio and how the story says he is a bare tiger, no longer clothed in his favorite stripes. I feel sad for Horatio and hope that at The End he will find a way to win back his stripes. I raise my hand.

Because Horatio traded his stripes to try on Ruggles the rhinoceros' tusks, I say. And now Ruggles doesn't want to trade back. Horatio has to think of a way to get Ruggles to. . . .

"OK, Sharon," Miss Pearl says, "but now let's continue with the story."

December 15, 1967 • It is bathroom time. Miss Pearl sends all of us children to use the boys and girls rooms. Me and Otte wash our hands really clean. I am not shy with Otte. She is my best friend at school. Otte is from India. She's really small. Shorter than me, and I'm not big.

The soap bubbles feel so good on our hands. We watch the bubbles get smaller and smaller when we hold them between our palms. That's a word Mommy taught me. Then, put more soap on and rub our hands together really hard. More bubbles. All of a sudden we look up and see Miss Pearl. She's mad. I look around the bathroom. There's no one but me and Otte. All the other kids are gone. I don't know how long we have been in here, but it must be a long time, because now we are in trouble.

I'm sorry. I didn't mean to be bad. The teacher looks so angry. She thinks me and Otte are bad girls. How can I tell her we're not? That we were just playing with the soap. See, look how big a bubble you can make.

She drags us out of the bathroom. Takes us back to our class. What is she doing? Miss Pearl makes Otte stand in the corner of our classroom. All the kids are staring at us. It is really quiet. What about me? Where are you taking me? We come to another class. With kids I've never seen before. Miss Pearl stands there talking to the teacher. Then she puts me in the corner of this other class. All the children are staring at me. I try to stand there tall. I fix my skirt and open my eyes really wide so the tears won't fall out where they can see them. Cry on the inside. I'm not bad. The kids keep staring, and the teacher says, "Come on children, let's get back to work." In this corner I feel so sad. My whole me hurts. I can't keep this tear in. I feel it sliding down my face. Then another. I turn my back to the class and cry. I'm not bad. I cry so hard. I don't remember what happened the rest of the day.

May 1, 1968 • Today is Maypole Day. It is so beautiful. There is a tall maypole in the middle of the school park, in the center of all these trees and lots of green grass that looks like Mommy's velvet dress in her closet at home. The ribbons are flying and it's yellow hot and Mommy and Daddy are here. Sherry and me laugh and dance in our brown dresses with white daisies. My eyes sting, because today the air and sun and ribbons and grass and we . . . are all free.

Can every day be Maypole Day?

June 1, 1968 • Saturday, Mommy takes us to a carnival way out on Long Island. On the way, Sherry makes voices of different characters on TV. Mommy, Daddy and I love her voices. Daddy always asks her to imitate Mutley, the funny dog, laughing. When she does, it sounds just like him.

At the carnival the rides, tents, cotton candy and lemonade keep us racing all over. We want to see everything! Then we smell the animals. As soon as Sherry spots them, she runs toward the camel. She only wants to ride him. She's not afraid to sit way up on top, at his hump. I choose the elephant. He is so wide that four kids can ride him at one time.

On the way back home, Sherry talks about the camel. Her ride sounded like more fun than the elephant, but I was kind of scared to go up so high. She's not afraid of anything. Sherry never makes fun of me, though. She does the Mutley laugh for me. I pat Mutley on the head and we count red cars out the window.

Lying in bed at night, I think again about shy.

With Sherry, Mommy and Daddy, I love talking and laughing. And with my friends. But sometimes, I just feel not sure with people I don't know. I have all these thoughts and feelings in my head that take up most of the space. I'm not sure if I can share them.

June 11, 1968 • We live in Rochdale Village. In Jamaica, Queens. Mommy says they are called co-op apartment buildings. Rochdale has more buildings than almost anyplace else in Queens, or in all of New York. Twenty buildings. Two malls. Parks. Tennis courts. And schools. In September I will start kindergarten at P.S. 30.

At home in our apartment building, Building 10, I play with my friend Mark. We take the school bus together. Yesterday his grandmother picked him up from the bus instead of his mommy. I was playing with Mark, but his grandmother told me to get away from them. She said mean things to me that I don't understand. I will ask Mommy.

Mommy says that Mark's grandmother sees us differently. That Mark's grandmother was saying that I am colored and Mark is Jewish, so she didn't want Mark and me to play together. She says Mark's grandmother also used a bad word to me.

I don't understand, so I ask Mommy. I'm not Jewish?

"We are colored," Mommy explains.

What is colored? I ask her. I hold out my hands to her. See, my hands look the same color as Mark's.

"There are different races of people in this country and in the world. Colored is what many people in this world are. You can be colored and have yellow skin, brown skin, or black skin," Mommy says.

I try hard to understand. I didn't know we were different. Is Mark still my friend? I hope so.

September 10, 1968 • Kindergarten. Tomorrow I start the morning class, even though the other kids who are born in July, like me, are in the afternoon kindergarten. I don't understand all of it, but Mommy says I need to be in the morning class because that's the group that will be the smart class for first grade. She wanted me changed out of the afternoon class where I went at first. I heard her telling the teacher that I can keep up with the older children in the morning kindergarten.

Mommy is a teacher. She teaches junior high school science and reading. She says she has been teaching since before I was born. Since before she even finished college. She has taught little kids like me and bigger kids, like she does now.

At home, Mommy teaches Sherry and me all the time. She uses readers for big kids. And books about science and history. She says schools don't teach geography anymore the way they did when she was a kid. So she will teach us at home. Geography is studying maps and stuff like that. It's kind of boring. But I love history, thinking about people who were once little kids like me. I like to look at their pictures when they were young.

"What do you think about when you see these photographs?" Mommy asks me.

I imagine them all grown up, and what they did with their lives, I say, kind of quiet. Mommy smiles and asks me another question that makes me think hard.

September 13, 1968 • I like my morning kindergarten class and my teacher, Miss Emma. It's not tough after all. It's fun.

After class every day, Daddy picks me up and I tell him about school. We walk to the bus stop on Bedell Street from my classroom in a building way on the other side of Rochdale. He holds my hand all the way there.

"How was school today, Bugs Barron?" Daddy asks me. He call me Bugs Barron and Sherry, Bugs Berry. Or else he calls us both Bugsy for short.

Today, we learned about the planets! I tell Daddy, kind of yelling, cause I liked the lesson so much.

"My favorite planet is Saturn," Daddy says with a laugh. "It's mysterious, and I like all the rings around it."

Daddy takes me to Benson's Burgers on the corner of Merrick Boulevard, right at the stop where we get off the bus to go to the baby sitter. I can eat two hamburgers when I am super hungry. This is my special time with Daddy, no one here but the two of us.

We walk to Mrs. Terranz's, the baby sitter's house. Sherry is there already, back from nursery school. She's always really excited to see me. After Daddy drops me off, he takes the train to work. We won't see him until late tonight. I give him a kiss goodbye and run into the playroom.

I'm not shy with Mrs. Teranz's children, Zora and Victor. But I'm different when other kids come around that I don't know. Like Zora's cousins or some of Victor's friends.

May 19, 1968 • Today I wrote a poem! Not just in my head. I actually wrote it down on paper.

The sky is so blue
Do you know why?

I do not know
But I will find out why.
Someday. Maybe when I die.
Well. Anyway.
I'm happy and that's all I need to know.

October 9, 1969 • We have special school notebooks. Black-and-white hard covers on them, and we write headings on the top of each page. Mine looks like this:

P.S. 30 Q   Sharon Simpson
Class 1-305   October 9, 1969

This year I get to go to school all day. Nine to three. In class we are learning how to write. I know how to write because Mommy and Daddy taught me.

Mrs. Looney is my teacher. What a crazy name. A lot of times Mrs. Looney is out sick. She is old with white hair. Even when she is there she doesn't say much. Mrs. Queen is our substitute teacher. She is really nice. She seems kind of like my own mommy. We have Mrs. Queen more than Mrs. Looney. I'm glad.

There is this boy named Christopher Corrin in my class who I really like. He wears rectangle glasses and has pretty brown-red skin. He doesn't talk to me much. I think maybe because I am shy, but that's OK, I like him anyway.

November 5, 1969 • I do my own hair now. I think I do it prettier than Mommy does. Sometimes I style Sherry's hair for her, too. I love being the big sister and taking care of my sister. When she sits still long enough for me to do it, I do her hair really beautiful. Mommy always makes three pigtails and has me wear the third pigtail in the front hanging to one side. When I do my own hair, I let the third pigtail hang down the middle of my head, nice and long in the back.

Mommy says it makes my ears stick out with my hair back like that. Because I have a high forehead. What is a high forehead? A lot of space between my eyebrows and my hair? I don't care. I like the way it looks. I am wearing my hair like this for my class picture.

November 11, 1969 • Sherry and I are taking violin lessons at the school where Mommy teaches, Junior High School 8, on Linden Boulevard. We go there for the after-school program. We have our own violins. I love my violin and the beautiful velvet case it sits in. Sometimes, though, it gives me a headache when I squeak it while playing.

Mommy sews us dashikis to wear for the evening recital. Mine is gold with black-and-navy-and-green trim. Sherry's dashiki is in her favorite color, turquoise.

November 12, 1969 • Tonight is our special night . . . the recital. The stage is really big. All I can see are the lights shining in our faces as we perform. We kids are lined up, playing together. We sound pretty good. I am trying so hard not to mess up. I look over at Sherry standing next to me. She is smiling. I see where she is looking. She has spotted Daddy, Mommy, and Mommy's mom, Grandmother Thompson, in the audience. Now I see them, too. Sherry just waved with the hand that holds the bow! She doesn't mind, either, if anybody saw her do it. Oh, I missed that note; I'd better pay attention. I won't try the wave thing. I might miss.

December 24, 1969 • It's Christmas Eve! In our family, Christmas Eve is when we decorate the tree. Mommy pulls out all the decorations where they are stored in the top of the hall closet. There are even decorations from when she was a little girl. Gold stars that she and Uncle Louchy used to hang on their tree.

We get to stay up really late. We bake cookies for Santa and leave them out in the kitchen. Slice-and-Bake chocolate chips from me and sugar cookies from Sherry. We play "Silent Night" on the record player, and then Mommy and Daddy finally make Sherry and me go to bed.

Sherry peeks out the door, looking for Santa. Christmas Eve is about the only time when our bedroom door is closed. It is really hard to fall asleep. Outside our window, it is snowing. I love it when it snows on Christmas. Just like on TV.

December 25, 1969 • Morning! I feel Sherry shaking me to get out of bed. We race out to the living room. Under the Christmas tree are gifts, gifts, gifts! Dolls and games and arts and crafts sets and lots of clothes. Wow. There's a pair of skis for each of us. And long johns, just like pajamas. And ski pants, jackets, gloves, hats, and scarves.

"Let's practice," we shout at the same time. Up and down the hallway we ride on our skis. We are going skiing in January. How did Santa know?

There are beautiful new pairs of clip-on earrings, too. "You can wear them on special occasions," Mommy tells me.

I don't have pierced ears. Mommy says Grandmother Thompson didn't let her get hers pierced because you can get keloids. I try on the little butterfly earrings with my new pink nightgown. I dance around the foyer in front of the mirror. I look like I am in a fairy story.

Mommy has to force me to get dressed because it is time to go to Grandmother and Grandpop Simpson's house for Christmas dinner. Sherry has been playing with her new SST race-car, making it zip and roar all through the house. Mommy has to force her to get dressed, too.

Daddy has six brothers and a sister. They will all be there except for Uncle Charlie. He died as a young man in World War II from a bomb explosion. He was the oldest son. My uncles have lots of wives and children.

Grandpop got this big brown easy chair last year for Christmas. Sherry and I play in it and rock it back and forth when no one is looking. Sometimes, even when they are looking. Out of all our cousins, Joel and Christopher are our favorites. They do magic tricks for us. Even though they are teenagers, not grownups, they know how to make a penny disappear. And they talk to us, even though we're only little kids.

We always stay at the house until it is really late. I am getting sleepy, but I try to stay up and listen to everybody talking.

Uncle Ben is playing the piano, making up a funny song about the family while he plays. Most everybody in the family plays the piano. Grandmother is a music teacher. All the uncles still talk about how Cousin Joel performed in concerts when he was only four years old. There's this picture of him that Grandmother keeps of him in this tiny black suit in front of this huge piano. Daddy is really talented on the piano, too. He's the second youngest brother. It seems that most of his brothers talk more than he does. His brothers call him Kenny, not Ken like my mom calls him. It is hard to keep my eyes open. . . .

I stretch my eyes really wide to keep from falling asleep. Sherry laughs at how funny my face looks when I do that. I look around at our family. We are lots of different colors. My uncles, aunts, and cousins. Just like how Mommy said the world is. Grandmother showed Sherry and me her mother's picture. She came from Sweden a long, long time ago. Grandpop's family is from New York, where we live now.

Mommy is waking us up. It is time to go home. We fell asleep, after all. In Grandpop's big, brown easy chair.

February 10, 1970 • We are sitting at the kitchen table, drinking hot tea like we always do. Mommy, Sherry, and me. Laughing. "The students want to go on a trip to the Amish country," Mommy tells us. "Yea!" Sherry and I shout. That means we get to go, too. Sometimes Mommy takes us on special field trips with her class. She says even though we are much younger than her students, there is so much for us to see and learn that it's good to start early.

I love it when we sit in the kitchen telling the stories of our day. I think this is our favorite place in the house to be together. The telephone is ringing. It is always ringing. Mommy gets a lot of phone calls. One day I will, too.

Wait, I hear her say my name. It sounds like she is talking to my teacher. Sherry and I look at each other. Mommy takes so long on the phone.

Mommy says I have won a contest. We have to get dressed really fast because there is a big assembly at P.S. 30 main building, and I am going to receive an award. What contest? I don't remember. "For drawing a picture," Mommy explains.

Oh, now I remember the picture. I am so excited. I have won an art contest! I'm glad Sherry is coming too. Daddy is not home from work yet. He's a social worker. He works all the way in the South Bronx. It takes a long time to get there. I know because when they had a bazaar at his center, we all took the train there. It took four hours. Maybe it wasn't that long. I better ask Mommy. No, she says, it was two hours. Still long.

At school we sit in the audience until a teacher I have never seen before says into the microphone, "Sharon Simpson." I walk slowly up the steps to the middle of the stage. She shakes my hand and hands me a huge dictionary and a radio. She calls it a transistor radio. I love them both. My own dictionary. The transistor radio needs batteries. Mommy promises we will buy them tomorrow after school.

February 27, 1970 • I got this idea. I have decided to do my hair in an Afro. I see lots of people have them. I want one too. I wet my hair and rolled it up on curlers. This morning I worked on picking it with Daddy's Afro pick for a long time. Mommy teased it out for me a little bit to get rid of the patches that weren't Afroey enough. I let her do it, but I checked it all out in the mirror when she was done.

I was a little nervous, but school went OK. The kids didn't say too much. I guess it looks fine. Maybe I was worried for nothing.

Mommy and I go to pick up Sherry. Sherry is in nursery school, so she still goes to the baby sitter in the afternoon. Mrs. Terranz opens the door with Zora standing next to her.

As we stand in the doorway, Zora points her finger at me and begins to laugh. I leap into the house, pouncing on Zora and knocking us both down. Yelling something about don't laugh at me. Zora is much bigger than me, but it takes Mommy and Mrs. Terranz a few shocked minutes to pull me off. Sherry is standing there looking at me in surprise. Everybody is. Even Zora.

I don't know why I did it. I just got mad when she laughed at me, I try to explain on the heavy drive home. Sherry thinks I am silly. It is the first time I can remember hearing the word "sensitive." My mother says that's what I am, too sensitive.

March 16, 1970 • My Grandmother Thompson has passed away. She lived in Rochdale too. She moved here last year from New Jersey. Sherry and I would go over to her house and play. She even let us decorate her hair with tissue bows. We would spend lots of time with her and Mommy doing all sorts of fun things driving in the Volkswagen that takes us everywhere. Grandmother Thompson taught Spanish to grown-ups. She used to go on lots of trips, too, to places like France, Spain, and Puerto Rico. We would go the airport to meet her and pick her up. Before she got sick.

Mommy says that Grandmother had a bad thyroid condition when she was young. Because I've got big eyes and my throat is kind of swollen, they think maybe I have it, too. I think it is the bee sting I got on my throat when I was four. Mommy said Grandmother died of a heart attack, not from her thyroid. Now Grandmother is gone. But I know she is in heaven. Where is heaven? I wonder if I can see it if I stare straight up into the sky.

Mommy is so sad. She is lying on the edge of her side of the bed, crying. Sherry and I go into the room. It is dark. We stand there looking at Mommy, and we touch her arm. She kind of looks up at us, and then she keeps crying. Daddy is patting her head. We walk out of the room really quiet. We go into our room. We listen to my little transistor radio. We don't say anything.

Mommy has all these cards to send out to people about Grandmother dying. We also need groceries. We have been to the Rochdale Mall before by ourselves.

We hear Mommy say quietly, "I am teaching you girls early, just as my mother taught me."

She makes a list of what we should buy from the supermarket. First we are supposed to go to the post office and get a roll of $20 worth of stamps; each stamp costs 20 cents. She gives me a $100 bill. I know how to count the change because she taught me.

Sherry and I go to the mall. We always stick close together. Mommy told me to watch Sherry closely when we cross the street. I hold her hand tight when we do. Then, let her hand go and we walk, careful to step over all the cracks. Make walking a game. We make everything fun.

At the post office, I pay for the stamps with the $100 bill. I stand on my tiptoes to see the man at the counter. Sherry is right by my side, even though she can't see over the counter. She knows how to count too. He gives me my change and I put it all away in my purse after counting it. I say thank you and then we go. He looks at Sherry and me kind of strange. I don't know why. But we go to the market.

We buy everything on Mommy's list. Then we are allowed to choose a snack. We choose the vanilla-and-chocolate icing Entenmann's cake. Sherry likes the white icing and I like the chocolate, so whenever we get this cake, we are really careful how we cut the squares.

Finally, because we have done so well, I guess that Mommy won't mind if we get a slice of pizza. I buy us two pizza and soda combos. I eat the pizza so fast that it burns my mouth. Then we head home.

Mommy is very proud of us. We even get Mommy to smile. She doesn't mind that we got pizza. That was what you call a good judgment call. We are learning to make those as well as learning to go to the store and do stuff on our own.

July 2, 1970 • Our family is going to Disney World in Florida! We are driving all the way there from New York. It will take us three days. Sherry and I have our pillows and blankets spread out on the back seat of the car. I love these family trips. And I love driving places. Last summer we went to Canada. I never mind how long the car ride is. I love the feeling of going somewhere new, no matter how long it takes to get there.

We drive through many small towns; finally we stop for lunch at a little town in South Carolina.

Why are those people staring at us? That man looks kind of mean. Mommy quickly calls my name: "Sharon!" I catch up to her. She holds my hand tight and doesn't let go. I am glad when we get back to the car. I love riding in the car, but I don't always like stopping.

July 5, 1970 • Today I met Minnie Mouse. She is my favorite. I wanted to tell her how much I like her, but I didn't. I saw this little girl with red hair give Minnie a big hug. I wanted to, too. But I didn't. I thought about it, though. I thought about it hard. I am always thinking. Sometimes thinking hurts.

July 8, 1970 • Mommy injured her back. She pulled a muscle or a disc or something like that. She is in a lot of pain. I am sad to see her like that. But she says she is still having lots of fun. And she still plays with Sherry and me all the time. But she will have to fly home. Sherry is going to fly with her. It's Sherry's first plane ride. I've never flown before, either.

Since I am the oldest, I will drive back with Daddy. I'm glad I know how to pack my own stuff and do my hair. It will be different driving without Mommy and Sherry. I'll miss them. But I am the big sister and I will drive back home with Daddy. Keep him company. Kind of taking care of each other. I am excited. We are going to stop at this place called South of the Border. I want to get a cowboy hat.

July 11, 1970 • Daddy and I drive all the way home to New York. It is fun. We talk a lot. I don't really remember about what. Just funny stuff.

We go to South of the Border. It's OK. It is just a big store with lots of stuff. Daddy lets me choose whatever I want. I get a piggy bank, and we buy some souvenirs for Mommy and Sherry. I don't mind when we leave. I like the car driving much better.

August 17, 1970 • We just got home from the Bronx Zoo. We have had lots of fun this summer. We went to plays and movies and flower parks and rodeos. For three weeks we went to day camp, where they have the best turkey sandwiches in the world. Even though I broke my arm the last week, when I fell trying to run and let my group know that the bus had arrived, I loved camp.

We don't play outside much because we are always going places. I don't like to play outside anyway, cause the kids think we are different. At least that's what it feels like. They asked Mommy if we are from California, because they say we talk funny. And somebody always wants to fight somebody else.

I like to play in the house when we do play. Sherry and I make up all these games. We do our levitating body magic trick, using blankets and fake legs made out of our ski poles. We have all our dolls go to summer camp. We are a horse and cowboy. We are Oliver Twist and the Artful Dodger.

We make bouk-a-shouk.

September 14, 1970 • Finally, I am in the big main school building of P.S. 30. It stands on the corner of Bedell Street. Made of light colored brick, it is huge, and the classes go all the way up to fifth grade. There are lots of classes in each grade.

For the second grade there are about 12 classes. Most of the kids from my first grade are all still together. I guess Mommy was right about tracking, because we are class one in our grade.

My teacher is Mrs. Weissman. She is "creative." She is teaching us lots of new words. My favorites are "conservation" and "pollution." I sing them on the way to school. I keep thinking it would be fun to make a kid's magazine with stories using all the new things we are learning in class.

I love doing dioramas on stories that we read and imagining myself in the stories as well. I close my eyes and see Christopher and me getting married. I still like him a lot, but he doesn't talk to me much.

September 22, 1970 • At lunch we go to the little schoolyard for the younger kids. Lately close to the end of the period, soon before the bell rings, some of the children have started making fun of me. It's this one big group of girls from my class.

Usually I am over on the side playing games with Jodi Steiner, who has been my best friend since first grade. Jodi is quiet, too. But then the girls come over and start making fun of me. I try to ignore them, and then I tell them to leave me alone. Still sooner or later, one of them will come up really close to me and push me.

I can't just run away; then I wouldn't like me anymore. Why don't they like me, though? I swear I didn't do anything to Lisa or Joanna or Denise or Melinda. Still, each day they come over.

Denise hits me hard. So I hit her back, and we start fighting. I can't see anything, just my arms moving and feeling her pulling my hair and clothes as I swing my arms and hear the kids yelling. Blowing her whistle, a school aide pulls us apart. Now we are in trouble.

"Sharon started it," the girls yell. Denise looks really mad and kind of shaken up. I don't know what I look like. The aides grab us by our collars and make us stand against the fence until the bell rings to end lunch period.

We are back in class. Every day, Mrs. Weissman has all the kids who the school aides reported during lunch stand in front of the class. We each have to tell why we got in trouble.

Denise and I had a fight, I say.

"Why?" the teacher asks me.

I don't know.

Some of the other girls stare hard at me. I stand up there and look straight ahead.

Next day, the same thing happens with Melinda. The day after that, Lisa. And then this super tough girl, Tawana. I don't know what to do. How to make it stop. I go into the bathroom and do my hair that got all mussed up in the fight, glad I know how to do it myself. I fix my clothes and then, again tell my story. I was in a fight today. . . .

This year is not fun like first grade. This year hurts.

October 14, 1970 • I am tired of trying to hide how I look after a fight. Today I leave my pigtails all messed up, my blouse pulled out, and my belt hanging. Mrs. Weissman talks to me in private, after lunch.

"You seem like a good girl, Sharon, but you must be doing something to be in all these fights."

I'm not bothering the girls, I tell her. I don't even play over there. I was skipping rope with Jodi in the corner of the yard. I feel a cry welling up, and I push it back down. Got to be strong. I've come this far.

I don't know why they pick on me. I can't keep the tear in any longer.

Finally, that afternoon, I tell my mother what has been happening at school. It is parent-teacher day and my mother talks to Mrs. Weissman. I don't know what she says, but Mrs. Weissman still believes me that I am not starting the fights. Maybe this can get better.

October 19, 1970 • On picture-taking day, Jodi stands in front of me in line. The school aide is walking down the line of kids, stopping at different ones of us to make sure we look fine for picture taking.

She passes by me and stops at Jodi. The aide combs and combs Jodi's long blond hair. We are all standing very close in line. The school aide has a big diamond ring on her hand.

Ow. I can't open my eye. Her ring scraped it. I'm afraid to open my eye.

They rush me to the office. The nurse looks at my eye and they call my mother at her school to come pick me up. I have to go to the eye doctor. Mrs. Weissman picks Alita to sit with me and keep me company in the office. Alita is very popular. She is friends with Denise and Tawana and Melinda. They like her and listen to her.

We have never really talked before. She is nice and fun to be with while I wait for my mom. I think about it, then I decide to tell her about my idea for a kid's magazine. "That's a great idea," Alita says, actually sounding excited. Talking to her, my eye doesn't hurt as bad. She tells me that all the kids are saying I am going to be blind, but she knows I'll be OK.

The eye doctor says I'll be fine in a few days. He gives my mom drops for my eye. The next day, Alita and I are friends.

I don't stand in front of the class after lunch anymore, because I haven't had any more fights.

July 16, 1971 • We see the plane, big and powerful, through the window of the airport. Sherry and I have on our peasant dresses, brown with tiny pink-and-white flowers for the trip. Usually we don't dress in the same clothes, like twins. But once in a while we wear the same outfits. I like it, but I think it gets on Sherry's nerves sometimes.

We are going to Europe for three whole weeks with our parents. The airline is Pan Am. It's stamped onto everything. Even the red blankets the stewardess gives each of us to snuggle under and keep warm. We want the flight to go on forever, even longer than the eight hours Mommy and Daddy said it would take to get to Spain.

We are part of a tour group, called Globers. We even get these blue vinyl Globers bags. I have packed mine with no help. In it are all my favorite things for the flight.

They say your ears pop when the flight takes off. I'm not sure what that means, but we are chewing our gum really hard so our ears will not pop. We saved the silver paper from the gum. I fold the paper into a really straight line, then stick it onto my teeth. Now I have braces. Sherry does the same thing. Her teeth stick out, so when she gets a little older, she really will get braces.

Lucky. Braces seem fun. But having your teeth stick out doesn't, because the kids call her bucktooth beaver. I think they are so mean when they do that. I never call my sister that mean name. Well, almost never.

I hate sitting on the inside of anything. Restaurants, bus seats, now planes. Since I am the oldest—I am 7 and Sherry is 5—I say I get the outside seat. Anyway, Sherry likes looking out the window.

July 18, 1971 • Spain is hot. The sun is really bright. I have to squint super hard when I look around. Especially when I am trying to focus on the camera with Mommy taking all these pictures of us everywhere. I keep trying to make funny faces.

"Smile," Mommy says to Sherry and me. I scrunch my face up really hard. I don't care what it looks like. It feels good. Mommy says, "Stop making those faces, Sharon. When you get older and look back at these pictures you'll be sorry you didn't smile." I don't care, I think. But I lessen the scrunch to a light frown and Mommy, sighing, snaps the picture. Sherry and I laugh and go back to our pig nose faces.

We are practicing pig nose faces for London. That will be the last city we visit. We are practicing our pig nose faces because we are going to make the Royal Guard laugh. Mommy and Daddy say they are not allowed to laugh no matter what. We have been practicing for a long time. We have lots of different pig nose faces. We pull our ears forward, stick our pinkies in our noses to push our noses up and pull down our eyes to make them really droopy. It is so funny. They'll have to laugh.

July 19, 1971 • Here in Spain we visit all these museums. One is this tiny place almost the size of a corner grocery store back home. In it, though, are skulls of monks who passed away thousands of years ago. It is scary, and I hold on tight to the back of

Mommy's poncho. It is very dark in there. When we get back into the light outside, it feels like a different world.

We go shopping and buy Mommy lots of beautiful suede shoes. I wish I could get some, but they are ladies' shoes. Mommy and Daddy let Sherry and me each pick out a doll for our souvenir doll collection from around the world. I get this beautiful flamenco dancer, or is she a princess? She is all dressed in black and yellow with a fan and a long veil in the back. Sherry gets a pink doll. I like hers too, but I like mine better.

Tomorrow we leave for Italy.

July 20, 1971 • Our room in Rome is really nice and private. It is connected to Mommy and Daddy's room through a door. We feel really grown up to have our own hotel room. Today we break the toilet seat, trying to see our pig nose faces in the bathroom mirror.

Mommy and Daddy aren't too mad, but they tell us to be more careful. The food here is delicious. I have lots of spaghetti sauce and spaghetti, but Sherry, who only likes hot dogs, french fries, chocolate milk, and not much else, eats spaghetti with butter. Boy, is she missing out. I do miss breakfast back home. Here it's all rolls and juice; they call it a continental breakfast. Today we visited this place called the Coliseum, where, thousands of years ago, men used to have to fight lions.

July 22, 1971 • We get to wear our new, light blue windbreakers to the top of Mount Pilatis, one of the highest mountains in Switzerland. We ride a tram up into the mountains to get to the very top. I hear Mommy say it is magnificent. I think so, too. You can walk really close to the edge and look over. Mommy is afraid and stays back. Daddy stands right at the edge and looks down. Sherry stands beside him. I stop a few steps before I am at the edge and stick my neck out really far to look down. Wow!

Walking through the town people stare at us. Daddy says at the hotel, they call us the brown family. But our name is Simpson, I say.

We went to a beautiful old jewelry store in town. This nice lady in a long dress tells Mommy and Daddy we are lovely girls. "So well behaved and well spoken," she says. "Are they twins?" People ask that a lot, even though I am taller than Sherry and, we think, we look different. But I like it when people ask the question. Because to me, being with Sherry feels like what I imagine it must feel to have a twin.

The lady gives Mommy two ivory pins as gifts for Sherry and me. Mommy says she will save them for us until we get older. Mommy is always saving things for us until we get older. Sometimes I wish she would let us wear it now. I won't break it.

July 24, 1971 • Sherry and I have a fight in our hotel room. We are arguing over who gets to sit on the inside of the plane when we fly back home (I guess Sherry is tired of the window seat), and somehow we get so mad that it turns into a fight. We are calling each other names and then we start hitting each other, hard.

Mommy runs in and pulls us off each other. She makes us sit apart and tells us to "calm down." Whenever we have a fight, Mommy tells us that we are lucky to have a sister and that we should appreciate that. Most of the time we do, but once in a while Sherry makes me really mad. Or I make her really mad, and then we argue and fight.

We can't stay mad at each other long, though. It's not fun when we don't talk to each other.

Want to go peek and watch the Globers dancing? I ask Sherry. "OK," she says, still serious. Then she adds, "maybe we can even practice our pig nose faces on them." We start to laugh; that's the way it is with us.

"I'm glad you girls are talking again," Daddy says. "But no pig nose faces at the Globers."

July 25, 1971 • The Globers wish me a happy birthday. At dinner, where I am served a hamburger with an egg on it (yuck), Mommy and Daddy have a slice of cake for me with a candle in it for dessert.

In Paris it has rained every day. We see this famous painting called the *Mona Lisa*. I don't think she is so pretty, but I like the way her eyes follow me wherever I stand. We also see this whole room of paintings by this artist van Gogh, who cut off his own ear. The paintings are dark and wild. I guess he must have been really upset. I feel sad for him. I try to imagine it. The nineteenth century, that is so long ago. His pictures are still here.

July 29, 1971 • They don't laugh. The Royal Guard don't think we are funny. We make the pig nose faces over and over again. All of our best ones. But they don't work. The guards never laugh. Not even the guard that looks kind of like Cousin Joel. Mommy and Daddy laugh, though. And some of the people around us. Oh well, we sure have fun. I like London anyway. And now we have great pig nose faces to take back home and teach our friends.

July 30, 1971 • I have a bad cold and can't go shopping with Mommy and Sherry. But Daddy is staying with me at the hotel. We play chess in the lobby by making chess pieces out of different items on the table, like matchbooks and salt shakers.

Mommy and Sherry pick out a new outfit for me from Harrods, with a long maroon vest, pants, and a turtleneck!

Sherry's outfit is blue. Here in London it is getting cold already, like back-to-school weather.

August 1, 1971 • The theater is very old and beautiful. *Fiddler on the Roof* is the most amazing play I have ever seen. Sherry and I love the story of the five sisters. Mommy and Daddy buy the *Fiddler on the Roof* album. I can't stop singing the songs in my head. I can't wait till we get home so that Sherry and I can act them out. I get to wear my new outfit. It feels kind of hot in the theater, but it is cold outside. I insist that Mommy take my picture with my cool new sunglasses. I even smile right for her. Tomorrow we go home.

In the taxi on the way back to our hotel, Mommy says how glad she is that they brought Sherry and me on the trip. "It doesn't matter what some of our friends said, I know the girls aren't too young to remember this. They'll never forget it."

September 13, 1971 • Sherry's first day back to school from summer vacation, the teacher says she lied. Each child gets to stand in front of the class and tell what they did for the summer. Sherry tells about our trip to Europe. She even remembers how many thousands of feet above sea level Mount Pilatis is. The teacher tells her to stop making up stories, that she didn't really go to Switzerland.

I hear Mommy on the phone talking to Mrs. Garnier, Sherry's teacher. I hear her say that my sister told the truth and how dare Mrs. Garnier assume that Sherry couldn't possibly have gone to Europe.

Sherry tells me that in class, she insisted that what she said was true, that she had gone to Europe and stood high on the ridge of Mount Pilatis. I am proud of my sister. She knows how to stand up for herself.

Sherry is sad that the teacher didn't believe her. I give her a hug, and we do some close-mouth exercises. We do close-mouth exercises so that Sherry can practice closing her mouth over her teeth. First I show her how to do it, then it's her turn. She tries really hard. We are working on this until enough of her baby teeth fall out to get braces. After our exercises, we whip up a special batch of bouk-a-shouk.

Sherry and I don't go to the same school. Sherry goes to a private school in Jamaica Estates. There are a lot of big, beautiful homes and mansions right near the school. I go to a public school in our neighborhood. Mommy says we each go to the school that is right for us to attend and where we need to be. That's OK with me. It's OK with Sherry, too.

October 4, 1971 • I am having fun now that I am in third grade! Alita and I are still good friends. I get along OK with the other girls now, too. Jodi's family moved out to Long Island this summer. I miss her.

In the morning, I walk to Alita's building and wait for her and Mrs. Madison, in their lobby. Her mom teaches fifth grade. Then we all walk to school together. It is fun to walk with Alita. I am always early. Some days they are late, but I wait anyway. One day we are even late for school. Good thing Mrs. Madison is there. Most days though, we have time to play in the yard before class.

December 14, 1971 • Our teacher this year, Mrs. Salmon, has traveled to lots of countries in Africa. She teaches us about them. At playtime in class, she plays this singer, James Brown, and the class has a Soul Train line. Some of the kids, like Freddie, do the funky chicken and dance on the floor. I feel super shy. I don't know how to dance. Not like this anyway. Sherry and I take jazz and African dance lessons with Mrs. Walker at the Community Center. I don't think that kind of dancing would work here, even though I like it better. The kids would laugh.

June 22, 1972 • This summer I am going to sleep-away camp, three whole weeks. The camp that Alita goes to, Camp Sokawow. I am so excited. I am also nervous. It will be my first big time away from Mommy, Daddy, and Sherry. I am going to miss them. I have my own trunk, sleeping bag, and everything. I love packing. Mommy and I are packing my trunk together. She shows me how to place everything really neatly. I will have my birthday at camp. There is a Visiting Sunday in the middle of my three-week stay, when the families come have a picnic and see their children.

July 5, 1972 • I'm worried. What if I don't really like camp?

July 7, 1972 • Mommy and Daddy promise that if I really hate it, they will let me come home at Visiting Sunday. I'm so relieved.

July 8, 1972 • I hug Sherry good-bye so hard. We have never ever been apart before. Me and my little sister. It's raining hard as the bus pulls off. I can barely see my family through the window. I am glad I have a notebook to write in. I hold it tightly on my lap, on top of my wet raincoat.

Late night
I think the wood cabins are really cool. I even get a top bunk. With my flashlight on under the covers, I can write no matter how late it is. I am sad, though, because I am not in Alita's unit. Since I turn nine while I am at camp, and Alita won't turn nine until September, they put me in the next unit. Pretty much everyone is older and bigger than I am.

July 14, 1972 • I like my cabin mates. We have fun. My counselor's name is Donna. Each cabin gets a counselor who takes care of the kids and organizes all the activities for her cabin's campers. We know she has a boyfriend who is a counselor for Panuawa, the older boys' unit.

"Where's Donna?" we are always asking each other. The girls in the other cabins learn to make juice from berries, go on hikes, have special BBQ dinners at the unit house, but Donna is hardly ever around. I wish I were in another cabin.

Yesterday, Colette in my cabin cut her arm on this rusty nail on the door. We were all terrified, but Donna wasn't there. Colette ran screaming, with the rest of us behind her, to Cabin Five. Luckily, the nice counselor, Lydia, took Colette to the infirmary.

We are trying to make our own fun, my friends and I, but it is lonely sitting in the cabin after morning swim. The other counselors don't notice. Each day when we walk to swimming, the boys' units line up by the side of the lake and yell at us in our swimsuits. Why are they doing that? I am only a little kid. I don't like this camp. I wish I were home with Sherry playing space games with our Billy Blast Off set.

July 23, 1972 • Finally, after two boring and scary weeks, it's Visiting Sunday!

I pack my whole trunk just the way Mommy taught me. I even pack my toothbrush after I use it this morning. I hug my friends good-bye. I don't see Donna. I am going home!

Sherry! Sherry and I run into each other's arms. It is a reunion. They brought a great picnic lunch and birthday surprises for me. A beautiful birthday cake and party bags for all my cabin mates. Sherry tells me how she put all the little marshmallows on the cake. It looks great! I take them to see my cabin. See how I am packed and ready, I smile.

They say I have to stay. I can't come home.

I don't understand. It was a promise. Why did you tell me I could leave?

"You're staying," they say again. And they unpack my things. Hang my raincoat back up. Put my washbasin back into the cupboard. Unroll the sleeping bag I'd struggled to tightly pack and place it back on my bunk.

Sherry and I look at each other. Sherry looks sad. I start crying, and I can't stop. I cry as they set up my birthday cake for my cabin friends and when they give me my cards and gift. Please don't leave me here, I beg. First in my head. And then out loud. It's time for them to leave. I am still crying, harder and harder. They hug me good-bye. I do not hug them, tears still rolling down my face. My family leaves. Sherry looks back.

My cabin mates think the cake is delicious. "Whose birthday is it?" some parents ask as they return their daughter to the cabin. The girls point to me where I am crying in my bunk.

I get mad that I am still here. It's not fair. Why did they tell me I could leave if it wasn't true? I rip up my birthday card, write mean messages like "I hate you" on it, and put it in one of the preaddressed envelopes Mommy made for me. I leave it at the unit house for mail pickup.

Later, I calm down. I race back to get the letter. It is gone. The mail has gone out.

I am sad. I shouldn't have lost my temper. Mommy is always warning me that I've got to learn to control my temper.

And they shouldn't have promised to let me come home if they didn't mean it. I miss Sherry.

August 5, 1972 • Sherry tells me it was her card I ripped up. Sherry, I am so sorry, I didn't realize it, I was so upset. Mommy is sorry, too. Daddy and I don't talk about it at all. They are glad to have me home.

August 12, 1972 • Sherry and I play with our dolls. We create a new world for them. Today they are going to college. We have special voices we make for each of the dolls. They each have their own personality. Christina and Big Tough Susan get in an argument over a class project. Thumbalina, we call her Thumby, helps them solve it. So does Johnny, Thumby's brother. Johnny is Sherry's doll; she gave him (he used to be Thumbalina too) a haircut so he could be the boy. Johnny and Thumby are our favorites, but we don't let the other dolls know that; we treat them all really fairly.

October 10, 1972 • I love to write. Alita and I are working on our kid's magazine. We showed it to Mrs. Bass and she says it's really good.

Every year at P.S. 30, we have International Day. Each class is a different country, and we dress up in costumes of that native land. This year we are Ireland. I get to wear a shamrock headband.

I still like Christopher Corrin. At lunchtime, my friends and I skip eating so that we can get a swing. The big kids, kids even from the nearby junior high school, hang out on the big swings. We go on the little swings, but we sit on top of the baby bar. I close my eyes and dream of marrying Christopher Corrin. He still doesn't talk to me much. That's OK, because I like Daniel Larson, too, and we sit next to each other in class.

December 4, 1972 • Some of the kids say bad words to each other. Curse words. I don't like those kinds of words. I don't feel good even thinking them, so I don't use them. Only last week, this boy Eric was chasing me and I was running and I yelled this curse word—it was "fuck"—to see how it felt. I turned around and there was

Daddy. He had come up to the school to surprise me. I don't know if he heard me or not. But I will not say a bad word again. I didn't like it. It's not me. I don't care if some of the other kids say them.

February 18, 1973 • Mommy is finally letting me use the journal that Aunt Saraan bought for me in Spain. It is so pretty, dark green with gold on the cover.

Now I am going to write all my thoughts in it. The ones that keep bouncing around in my head and that I wrote on loose-leaf paper before.

I write my new poem on the first page:

A YOUNG CHILD'S DREAM
Every child needs some fun.
A boy might like to play with a toy gun.
Every child needs some love.
A girl might like a rubber dove.
The dove is the symbol for love and peace
Such things deserve a celebration feast.
The gun is the symbol for war, which stands
For the hate of the poor to me,
But we the people, we children
Can grow up to be a better generation.
I believe one day the gun will run
From the beautiful dove, meaning love.

April 6, 1973 • On the weekends, my father plays ball, baseball. Every weekend, our family goes to the ball park on Lennox and 145th Street in the city. The best thing about it for Sherry and me is going to Kentucky Fried or spicy Kansas Fried Chicken. We play in the playground there and get really dirty. At the end of the games, everybody goes to this place called Gene's Bar. It's really dark. The jukebox plays, and the adults laugh and talk and laugh some more. Sherry and I get Shirley Temples, ginger ale with a cherry in a special glass. Daddy loves going to the ballpark. It seems like baseball is his favorite thing in the world to do.

April 7, 1973 • We have been going to classes at church. This year Sherry and I are going to make our first Holy Communion. We are becoming members of the Catholic church. Now we will go to our first confession and take communion for the first time. The priest says that now we have our own relationship with God.

April 8, 1973 • We wear beautiful white dresses and short veils.

It is dark in the confessional. I try to think of things to confess. I can't think of much. I tell the father how I tease my sister sometimes and that I am sorry.

I take communion for the first time. I have joined the church!

Afterwards we have a first Holy Communion celebration at home. Lots of friends and family are there. Daddy leaves early to go to the ballpark. People ask where he has gone. Mommy is upset. I am sorry Daddy left.

Sherry and I don't want to take off our dresses at the end of the night. They are so beautiful. We say our prayers.

April 10, 1973 • Yesterday I saw a sign at the library saying that there is a poetry reading scheduled for this weekend. I want to do it! Read my poetry.

I go back to the library with Mommy, and we talk to the librarian. She says it is a reading for mostly teenagers, but that they would be happy to have me. I am going to do it! Share my poetry. So far, I always read my poems to Mommy, Daddy, and Sherry and sometimes to teachers. Now I will have the chance to share them with more people, even older kids and parents.

April 14, 1973 • It is my turn to read. I feel Mommy and Sherry smiling at me. I stare once at my page and then at all the people sitting in the circle. I still feel shy. But more than that, I know this is a place where the thoughts that dance around in my head can be shared. People want to hear what I have to say. Even if it's different, or imaginative, or sensitive. I know my poem by heart. So I open my mouth, and the words come rolling out.

A SWEET SONG OF SUMMER
As cherry trees blossom
And the green grasses grow
And the birds they sing sweetly
Of flights to and fro
As summer approaches
And bees start to hum
These are the songs
that I like to hear sung

April 19, 1973 • Today I receive a letter from the librarian. It makes me feel so good and proud. I love poetry. I'm going to keep writing it forever.

Queens Borough Public Library
Dear Sharon,
A note of thanks for participating in our "Young Poets-Read-In" for National Library Week on April 14, 1973. Your poems were bright, lively, and light and you helped to make our day a success.
My best wishes for a bright future.
Again, thank you very much.

Sincerely,
Branch Librarian

August 10, 1973 • I have a decision to make. My first big decision, and Mommy says I am mature enough that I can decide for myself.

Sherry is transferring schools. She is leaving Vanden Country Day School to go to the public school P.S. 131, also in Jamaica Estates, down the block from Vanden. P.S. 131 is one of the best-rated schools in New York City. When you graduate from 131 you go to Ryan Junior High School, which is also highly ranked.

The question is, do I want to transfer schools too? Mommy says that for me to transfer to P.S. 131 now is an opportunity for me to continue to get an excellent education. That unfortunately the schools in our neighborhood are not providing the same level of education that they used to.

We sit on either side of Mommy as she goes on to explain to us that even within the two years after I started at P.S. 30, when it was time for Sherry to begin there, she had already observed that the education wasn't as strong. That's one of the reasons why she sent Sherry to Vanden. In my class, though, we were still getting great instruction, and she had wanted me to be at a school that wasn't as sheltered as Vanden because she hoped it would bring me out of my shell.

August 11, 1973 • I don't want to leave my friends. But Mommy says many of my friends will be leaving P.S. 30 anyway. Just as Jodie moved. I hear Mommy talking to Daddy about changes like white families leaving Rochdale and moving to Long Island. She is disappointed about not enough money from the school district and teachers not challenging students enough. She says it's hard to face, but it's true.

It is hard to choose. But I think about what the future holds. Future is a strange word. But I am excited about it. I also trust my mom's opinion. I remember that a lot of my classmates have been leaving already. Plus I am kind of scared to go to the junior high school near P.S. 30. I have heard from kids that it is very rough.

I don't really think about my friends' race or color. I have black friends and white friends and friends of different races. Nowadays, we say black, not colored like when I was a little kid. But I know that if I go to P.S. 131, I will be one of the only black children there. I wonder if it will make a difference.

I wrote another poem!

BLACK MEANS

Black is a tea, a color and me
Black means as black, as black as can be
Black means the night and the stars that shine so bright
Black means beautiful
As beautiful as white
Black is a tea, a color and me.

August 30, 1973 • Sherry and I will be going to P.S. 131 in September. My mother had to fight to get me put in the number one class on the grade. There are only two classes on each grade, really different from twelve classes at P.S. 30. Because I am coming from another neighborhood, the principal didn't want to put me in the top class.

"My daughters will be an asset to this school," my mom told her.

Sherry and I are both assigned to class one in our grade. We are going to school together! We will have to travel to get to school. Take the city bus. I think it will be worth it.

I am writing more and more in my journal. When I think and feel things strongly inside, I write.

THE DAY

As days turn into nights
And nights turn into days,
The day will break
And the sky will change
And I see that familiar light.
The rays from the sun shine down
They land upon the ground
The rainbow shows above the sky so clear and radiant.
I understand and now I see
I love this world
And the peace it brings
I love this day
With each new light
With each new dream
With each new hope
A day will be.

Pack Heart

I PLACE HEART IN MY BAG FOR LIFE'S JOURNEY.

In those shining moments, like sharing my poem, and in my darker moments, feeling alone and betrayed at camp, it was Heart that emerged . . . and saw me through.

Heart, that unique brand of empathy, courage and spirit all rolled into one, which comes from deep within.

Heart, my young self discovered. It rose to the surface, despite my fears of being too vulnerable or too sensitive. An opening of my spirit to what life gives me and to what I can give life.

When you are a little kid, it's all so new, and there you are trying to figure out and make sense, not just of life, but of who you are. To me, it is Heart that enables one to truly live each experience. Whatever it is. To live it to its fullest. Even when the going gets tough, not shutting down my emotions, but feeling them, with all the joys, hurts and the myriad stuff that lies in between.

Packing Heart is what I got from those awakening years. And though there are moments when it hurts to let my heart passionately pump, I have no regrets, that so early in life, that little girl made this choice.

When new adventures come, with Heart in my bag, I don't lose my capacity for empathy, for passion, for courage . . . all the qualities the heart will pump through the body, when we free it to be the vital organ it was created to be. Packing Heart lets me be gloriously, painfully, dramatically alive.

2

Girl Children Traveling the Mystical Road to Becoming Young Women

November 13, 1974 • "GIRLS! Girls. Wake up," I hear Mommy calling. Is it morning already? It feels so good in bed. I don't want to get up. Please don't interrupt this great dream.

But then I hear what Mommy's saying. "It's snowing." The first snow of winter.

That makes me jump out of bed. I get up and run to join Sherry, who's already gazing out the kitchen window. It's the best window for looking out and seeing the snow. The kitchen is warm from the heat Mommy turned on when she got up this morning. I can smell coffee, and I see that, even this early, the ground is completely covered with snow.

Sherry and I race to the hall closet where all the winter gear is kept; even the sled and our skis fit in there. We dig out our boots. Not the pretty black leather ones but the big rubber ones that fit over our shoes. It's that kind of weather.

Today the Q5AB bus takes forever to come. That's the problem with the city bus; it takes awhile, especially in weather like this. It's been a year now since Sherry and I started P.S. 131, so we are used to it.

We wait for the bus so long that it gets really crowded at the bus stop. We see the tall man who owns a big dog named Kunta, the lady who always stops and talks to Mommy at the mailbox, and a lot of other people we don't recognize.

To make the time pass faster, we play one of our Sharon and Sherry games. We dream up stories about what each person's evening was like the night before. We laugh and have fun with these visions. The bus still isn't here. It's freezing. So then I try to remember my dream from earlier this morning. But all I can remember is: I'm standing in front of a lot of people and singing this song with the most beautiful words I've ever heard. I search my mind for the words, but I can't find them. So I hold onto the good feeling that the words gave me.

Finally in the distance, we spot the bus, making its way slowly toward our stop. We are so cold by then that we don't care whether we'll get a seat or not; we just want the bus to arrive. It's packed with people. We are small and manage to squeeze in. It's going to be a long twenty minutes. Still, at least it's warm. Today we transfer buses to go up the hill to school. We won't try to walk; it's way too cold.

Sometimes we get a lift with Mommy to school. She is now teaching at Ida B. Wells School, right on Jamaica Avenue, only about fifteen minutes from P.S.131. It's a school for pregnant girls. Mommy teaches English there. She also does a lot of counseling. The students think she is cool and understanding. I think so too, because I can talk to Mommy about anything. Except, I can't imagine going to a school for pregnant girls. Some of the girls there are only a little bit older than I, like thirteen years old. They are having babies. I haven't even gotten my period yet. I wonder what that feels like.

November 15, 1974 • It feels funny to be in sixth grade and the senior class in the school. This year we graduate. We are finally the big kids.

Our teacher, Mr. Valmont, is always teasing different kids about going together. Even kids that really aren't! He just makes couples up. Like Chad Linwood and Tracy Larimer. Even though they say they hate each other and Tracy is really going with Corey, Mr. Valmont does it anyway. We think it's really funny, but sometimes Crystal and I think he pushes it.

Crystal is one of my closest new friends here. She is really cool and always knows what to say. She was one of my first friends in this school. She came over to me at lunch and asked me questions about myself. She talked to me about stuff that really matters, right away. Like what do I think the reason is our teacher doesn't let us girls play punch ball. We tried to figure out why, and finally decided to go and ask him. But he just laughed and wouldn't answer. I like having a friend that also has lots of questions . . . and looks for answers.

November 18, 1974 • I love to sing songs in my head and on the school bus when we go on a field trip. Today we went to the Museum of Modern Art. I love this song that is out called "Billy, Don't Be a Hero," about the war. I know all the words. Billy's girlfriend sings the song. It is really beautiful and really sad.

Coming home from the museum, "Billy, Don't Be a Hero" comes on again. When it is on the radio, I get really quiet and let all the kids go on talking around me. But I can see Billy trapped on the hillside, the battle raging all around. And Billy saves the men, but he dies. And his girlfriend is singing come back to me. But he's never coming back. And he's a hero. And every time I hear the song, Billy is alive again, and I get to relive with him and his girlfriend them being happy together and Billy going off to war and then Billy dying a hero and his girlfriend missing him.

I know it sounds crazy, but I miss Billy too.

At school this afternoon, a big group of us walk down the hill to the buses to go home, those of us who don't live in Jamaica Estates. We have lots of fun walking down the hill together and laughing and talking. We talk about boys and junior high coming up soon, what it's going to be like, and the silly stuff that happens in class, or that parents do. Crystal always has funny stories about the dumb stuff her mom does. She and her mom and older brother, Winston, don't get along very well, so Crystal and Winston live with their grandmother. Their mother lives in the city. Crystal gets along much better with her dad, but he doesn't live with them, either. He lives in the Bronx. Crystal and some of the other girls have kissed boys before. I never have. When they talk, I don't say that, I just listen.

Sherry and I take the bus home. It seems as though it comes faster in the afternoon. Maybe it's because we don't miss it as much because we are hanging out with our friends.

November 19, 1974 • We are getting much more schoolwork than before. We have research projects on different famous people in history. Mommy and Daddy bought a set of encyclopedias that I love. These books have everything I could ever want to know about anything. It seems like. I like them much better than the old almanac we have been using.

At lunchtime, my friends and I bring a jump rope and play double dutch. I've become pretty good at it.

It is the turn of this girl in our class, Gwen. She jumps while we sing: "Ten, twenty, thirty, forty, fifty," and all of a sudden her dress flies up. Big pajama bloomers are what we see underneath. The kind that come with a shortie nightgown. It is so funny that we drop the rope, we're laughing so hard. Gwen seems embarrassed.

The next morning while I am dressing for school, I look for some of those bloomers in my pajama drawer, and I put them on underneath my dress.

Watch this, I tell my friends. I pull up my skirt, and there are the blue bloomers. Just like Gwen's. Everybody cracks up. Except Gwen.

As we are all laughing, I look at Gwen's face.

That was mean of me, I admit to myself. It felt good making everybody laugh, but now I feel bad for making fun of Gwen. I'm sorry, I tell her.

Gwen just looks at me with this sad kind of smile on her face and walks away.

I won't tease her again. It left both of us with different kinds of hurting. I'm sorry, I say again in my head. Somehow, I know it isn't enough.

November 20, 1974 • At home on TV, it is Dean Martin and Jerry Lewis week. Daddy and I love Dean Martin and Jerry Lewis. They are so funny. Daddy sets the TV up in the foyer near the big mirror where I love to sing. The movies don't come on until 11:30 P.M. But he lets me stay up every week night with him so that we can watch the movies together.

Wednesday night is *The Nutty Professor*. Last night was *Cinderfella*. The movie doesn't go off until after 1:00 in the morning. Mommy and Sherry have been asleep for quite a while, but Daddy and I stay up into the night, laughing.

November 22, 1974 • It's Girl Scout cookie season again. Right now Sherry and I are both Juniors, but next year, I become a Cadet. We go door-to-door. "Girl Scout cookies," we say. We go to all three sections of the building, thirteen floors each, eight apartments per floor. That's a lot of cookies.

We're tired when we get home from selling cookies. When we arrive, Mommy is on the telephone. When Mommy gets off the phone, the three of us laugh our way through dinner while Sherry acts out the story of our cookie selling. "Most of the people were really nice, and we sold a ton of cookies," she says. "But one man said, 'Get away from my door, I don't want no d—— cookies,' and we ran."

Sherry actually has pajamas that say, "And now for my next number!"

Sherry and I talk about our upcoming African dance recital with Mrs. Walker, and we hang out together. Then Sherry stops to do her homework. She's really good about making sure she completes her work. I read the Mills and Boom romance book I smuggled home, smuggled because I feel embarrassed for Mommy to see me reading a romance that has people kissing and stuff like that. I got the book from my friend Annie at school. Her family is from Trinidad, and that's where she gets these great romances. Annie says they are sort of like Harlequin Romances. I am going to read one of those soon, too. I love reading Mills and Boom romances. I can go to a totally different place in my mind. Most of the time the stories take place in far away places like Australia and even New Zealand. They are so passionate and romantic.

November 23, 1974 • Last night I stayed up all night reading this romance about Rosalind and Rowland. By the time I finished, the sun was coming up. I was so sleepy when Mommy tried to wake me up this morning. But it was worth it. What a great book. Someday, somebody is going to love me like that, I whisper to myself.

I will borrow another book from Annie.

November 27, 1974 • Mr. Valmont says that we kids are growing up. They held a short growing up education session with us where they showed us slides about reproduction and things like that. I like it better the way they talk about it in my book *Are You There God? It's Me, Margaret,* by Judy Blume.

"We must. We must. We must increase our bust." That's what the best friends in the book chant as they hang out in one girl's bedroom, moving their arms vigorously to get their breasts to grow. I glance shyly down at my own chest. Nothing much there yet, but I am not worrying about it. Growing my chest isn't what I spend most of my time thinking about.

Maybe it's just that I don't want to grow up so quickly. And breasts growing seems like such a big step in that direction. I like dreaming about some of the exciting parts of being all grown up, like marrying my love. But maybe I don't like thinking about all the in-between steps so much. I feel kind of weird because lots of my friends seem so focused on being grown.

December 2, 1974 • Monday morning, and once again, the bus is super-crowded. Sherry and I are lucky to have gotten seats and gotten them together. Usually if there is an elderly person around, we offer them our seats. There's nobody around like that today, so we sit back comfortably for the ride.

At the ten-minute mark right at the triangle church bus stop—I know because I always time it in my head—this lady stands in front of Sherry. She tells my sister to move over. Sherry looks up at her confused. "Move over," she orders Sherry. Sherry slides over. Now we are sharing my seat, and the mean lady has taken Sherry's seat. That's not fair, I think. She had no right to do that. It is supposed to be our choice if we want to give up our seats. That was my sister's seat, and this is mine. I sit there. Angry. When I get older, I will not treat people badly, especially not kids, just because they are little, I promise myself. Little Sherry presses up against my side, and we ride the rest of the bus ride in silence. Humiliated.

December 10, 1974 • We've been taking African dance classes from Mrs. Walker now for a few years. Every Tuesday, Sherry and I and our friends, Joyce and Toni, who are sisters and the same ages as us, go to dance class. "Contract release, contract release," Mrs. Walker reminds us. Junie, her son, plays the bongos for the class. Her daughter Keesha is in the older class that meets after us. She dances really well and can shake her body so much, it seems as though every single muscle is moving.

"Afunga alafia, ahshé, ashé," we chant as we dance.

December 16, 1974 • In class, Mr. Valmont has us make Christmas ornaments and dreidels for Hanukah. We sing about Christmas trees, Santa Claus and menorahs, too. Last year, Crystal told me there is no such thing as Santa. I figured that means maybe the Easter Bunny and even the tooth fairy aren't real, either.

December 23, 1974 • Daddy bought home a huge box last night. We thought it was a gingerbread house. Instead, when we opened the lid, inside was a little black puppy. We are afraid of dogs, Sherry, me, and even Mommy. But we also love them.

After many false starts, we are sticking with the name Pepper. Daddy says Pepper is a combination of Labrador retriever and cocker spaniel. He looks like a miniature Lab with extra floppy ears and a white nose.

We wear boots around the house so Pepper can't jump up and touch our legs. We play a game in which we release him from his chain in the kitchen, where he stays while we train him, and run to our parents' bedroom. He is too small to jump on the bed, so the idea is to beat him to the bed, then jump up so he can't catch us.

Rochdale Village doesn't allow dogs, so it is a good thing he doesn't bark too much. Daddy loves dogs. He always had one when he was a kid, and he just couldn't take not having one anymore. So now we have Pepper!

December 25, 1974 • Christmas Day.

Since Grandpop Simpson passed away last year, after a long year of missing Grandmother Simpson when she died, we aren't going to the house this Christmas. Even though Uncle Clarence lives there now. We will stay home and have Christmas here. I realize that with the recent passing of Great Grandmother Cheatam, Mommy's grandmother, I have no grandparents left, and I am only eleven. I miss them.

December 31, 1974 • Over the Christmas holiday, Sherry and I acted out scenes from *Fiddler on the Roof*. Ever since we saw the play in London, we have been reenacting scenes from it in our bedroom. We dress in flowing scarves and nightgowns, sweeping imaginary dusty wood floors and singing about our dream man from the third song on the album. We use Mommy's beautiful suede high heels as part of our show.

Mommy told me it was time to start using deodorant. Sherry laughed at me. Mommy told her, "Your day will come too."

January 7, 1975 • At home in our neighborhood, the local football team is the Riffles. Sherry and I are Rifflette cheerleaders. Each weekend during football season we take the Riffles bus all over Queens to different parks for the games. I don't understand football too well, but I love doing the cheers.

Every year in Queens there is a cheerleading competition. I've been picked as one of the team to appear in the competition on behalf of the Rifflettes. I'm really proud of this. Deep down inside, I feel that I may not be as cool as some of the other cheer-leaders, but when I tried out, I worked really hard on doing per-fect cartwheels, splits and dance steps. So here I am, part of the in-crowd that goes to competition. It's difficult to admit, but for this particular moment, it feels good.

The competition is at night in Jackson Heights. We arrive and see cheerleaders from all over, in a rainbow of colored uniforms. Our uniforms are red and white. Riffles colors. I love my uni-form, but I see our home sewn red skirts, and our white wool turtlenecks with the red felt letter "R" look homemade compared to the fancy uniforms of some of the other teams. Still we sing our hearts out, "We are the mighty Riffles!"

We don't win. Some of the girls are really upset. But I think it's OK that we didn't win. I think we tried hard and the pyramid of the team that won was really amazing. I think our song was great, though, and I loved our perfect entrance. I'm sorry some of our team is mad. I am proud of us.

January 10, 1975 • Crystal and I and a bunch of us girls from Mr. Valmont's class get invited to Leah Cohen's sleepover. She is the second shortest girl in the class. Her older sister, Barbara, is really cool. She is into the singing group Kiss and has her hair in a spiky black hairstyle like the band wears it. Her makeup looks like the Kiss poster too.

Leah's mom makes fruit health shakes for us for a snack, and unsalted sunflower seeds. It tastes OK. We have fun hanging out and talking about the boys in our class. Leah says that last week Tracy and Corey were making out when our class went to the Planetarium. I didn't see them do it. I don't find talking about the boys in our class as much fun as talking about Christopher Corrin used to be. Or Daniel Larson who I knew liked me. Mr. Valmont never matches me up with anybody, and there's nobody I can think to match me up with either. Plus I am still shy.

January 15, 1975 • It is Martin Luther King Jr.'s birthday. A lot of people feel that his birthday should be a holiday that our country celebrates, like George Washington's birthday or Veteran's Day. If we did celebrate his birthday like that, the schools would be closed. But they're not. My mom talks with some of the other black parents at P.S. 131. Some have decided to keep their children home from school that day. My parents decide to send Sherry and me to school. I feel kind of bad about this. Crystal stays home. So does Joyce.

Mr. Valmont has our class write about Martin Luther King. It makes me feel better that our class is doing something special to acknowledge this day.

I chose to write my piece as a poem:

HIS GOD WAS PEACE
Martin Luther King was a great man.
He was a leader for the Black people's stand
Martin Luther King had a dream
His love for his race was supreme
Martin Luther King loved his race and yet,
He loved all people in every respect
He wished for our people to sing strong and loud,
To sing strong and loud that we're black and we're proud
He taught us to love all human beings,
To march and to fight against all unjust feelings
As he preached for his people using all of his breath,
He prayed for the taste of desired success

He won the Nobel Peace Prize
For his kindness and love of great size
Martin Luther King was assassinated
Because he and his race were hated.
Murdered because of a cruel fate
He died in 1968
His love for his people was supreme
He was Martin Luther King with the greatest of dreams.

February 14, 1975 • This Valentine's Day, Sherry and I have decided to make a surprise party for Mommy and Daddy. To do something special for them. Usually, every holiday, even the little ones, Mommy plans special parties for us to celebrate.

This year, we go to the store and buy white cupcakes with red hearts on them, lots of Valentine's candy and cards and a Valentine's Day tablecloth, napkins and cups. We decorate the kitchen and then call them in and yell, "Surprise! Happy Valentine's Day!" We want to give this day a sense of romance.

March 8, 1975 • Sometimes on Saturdays, Mommy takes us bowling with some of her friends and their children. Sherry, Mommy and I are all left-handed. We bowl with our left hands; I don't know if that matters or not. I'm not bad at bowling, but when we took tennis lessons last summer, the teacher had a tough time teaching me left-handed, or maybe I was just spastic?

Today when we were crossing the street to go to McDonald's after bowling, we saw a stray dog. Valerie said, "He's not going to get me, Sharon. He's going to get you, because he only likes light meat."

Nobody heard what she said except me. I didn't think Valerie would say something like that. We've been friends for as long as I can remember.

What she said hurt. I told Mommy. Mommy said that she was surprised Valerie would say something like that. She didn't believe it was what Valerie's family was teaching her. She's learning it from somewhere. I just wish it didn't have to be like this. It makes me feel gross. I wonder what she was feeling when she said it.

March 15, 1975• Saturday mornings I make breakfast for Sherry and me. I make her pancakes just like she likes them, with the sides crinkling from the hot butter I pour directly in the center of the pan. I keep cooking them until she gets full.

Saturday nights we all gather in Mommy and Daddy's bedroom to watch the *Carol Burnett Show.* It's one of the times we all spend together.

Sherry's spot is lying in the middle of the bed between Mommy and Daddy while we watch the *Carol Burnett Show.* There is Sherry's cute little face, her hand reaching out to tickle the extra curly part in the back of Daddy's head. He has the choice hair to tickle in the family.

Recently Pepper learned to jump up onto the bed. That was also the day he stole my Saturday night spot resting in the curve of my mom's legs.

I carved out a new space at the foot of the bed with what's left of my favorite blanket.

March 18, 1875 • Walking down the hill after school is one of the most special times of day for our little group. Soon it will be spring, and we've begun to linger as we walk down the hill each afternoon. We shed our gloves and scarves when the sun is its hottest, and run, laugh, tease, and chase each other down the hill.

We stop at the Pizza Shop, right next to the bookstore that carries the latest new Harlequin Romances each month. Crystal and Annie have joined our Girl Scout troop, so on Fridays we all take the bus together to our Girl Scout meeting. Today though, I have a confession to make. We spent our Girl Scout dues on pizza.

April 4, 1975 • It's time to plan summer camp.

This year we are picking Camp Kaufman! Girl Scout Camp. We're signing up for the special biking unit. We are going with Joyce and Toni. No more Camp Sokowow for me. Once was enough.

Mommy, Sherry and I sit down to figure out how much camp costs. We always look at things like this together. Mommy has her checkbook out to send in the deposit to hold our space. She is looking confused. Sherry and I are sitting on either side of her, me on the left where I always sit, Sherry on the right. She keeps adding up her checks, but somehow her account is short. "There's no money in the account," she says. What about camp? I'm thinking. Oh my God, don't tell me we can't go. We made plans with Joyce and Toni; we figured it all out. What's wrong? I think all of this but I don't say it. I ask, what happened to the money, if you thought there was money in the account? Mommy keeps adding, adding, adding, but it always comes out the same. There is $600 missing.

April 5, 1975 • Tonight, the men from the ball team come to pick Daddy up for a special awards dinner. Mommy is upset and she's not going. Turns out, the $600 went into buying the trophies for the team. Daddy used one of Mommy's checks from her checking account and paid the trophy company, and signed Mommy's name. He didn't tell her. Why would Daddy do something like that? I don't know what we are going to do about camp. I'm not giving up! I know we will figure something out. Mommy says the men told her that even if Daddy told her she doesn't need to come, she should come; all the other wives are going to be there.

We say good-bye to Mommy and Daddy, and Sherry and I stay home and talk and watch television.

It's really late and Sherry is falling asleep. I pull out *Are You There God? It's Me, Margaret* and read my favorite parts over again.

April 7, 1975 • Mommy tells Daddy she has to have the money back. Daddy says he is giving it back, he just has to wait till payday. I hope Daddy really gives Mommy the money. I know she needs it. Plus, we really want to go to camp.

April 25, 1975 • I'm so relieved. Daddy gave Mommy the money back. Mommy can still pay her bills. And we are going to camp.

May 16, 1975 • Today when Sherry and I come out of school, Daddy is waiting. He walks down the hill with us.

He tells us that Mommy has been in a car accident. At first, we think he was kidding.

I don't know why we would think he would kid about a thing like that, but we don't believe him. Not at first. Then we realize he means it.

"Where is Mommy now?" we ask.

"At the hospital," Daddy says.

Mommy is able to come home tonight. You can still see the glass in her curly Afro. Turns out, her car broke down, right after she came over the bridge. A man, late on his way for work, hit her even though she was parked on the side. Her car was sent careening across the expressway after his car hit her. Then two other cars hit her as well. Mommy says, as she was thrown onto the floor of the car and able to see the sky, she had peace, but she knew she wanted to be able to stay here and take care of us, her girls. So she says God let her live. I hear her saying to Daddy that when the police arrived at the scene, they couldn't believe she had actually gotten out of her car alive, that the car was crushed beyond totaled.

I have come up with another new poem. This one is a song. I am not sure what it means, but I like it. I even made up a tune for it.

THE WARNING
(A Song)
She came from the place, where no one would go
She begged them to listen
But they didn't want to know
By the times, the things prophesied began to be so
She was back in the place
Where no one would go
The warning was not heeded
And now it's too late
All the people are gone
And that was their fate
But now all the story is so long ago
And she's still at the place
Where no one would go.

June 20, 1975 • At graduation, I receive the creative writing award. I also get an award for history. Crystal receives a perfect attendance award, and Joyce gets an award for her artwork. It's funny I can write, but my drawing is not very good anymore. I don't know what happened to my early talent since my award in first grade. It seems like my pictures haven't progressed much since then.

For graduation, I get to wear pantyhose and high-heeled white shoes! I feel so grown up. I wear my hair in curls, and our whole family goes out for a celebration dinner. Now it's on to Ryan Junior High School. Wow!

We leave for Camp Kaufman in July. I can't wait. I am so excited. In our unit, there will even be an overnight biking trip, with lots of hills to climb.

We are not taking a long family vacation this year. Mommy and Daddy say that money is really tight. We don't mind, though, because we are having fun playing outside with Alita and friends from her building. Even though we don't go to the same school anymore, we still hang out together and are now in Cadets together. Alita is starting junior high school, too. She transferred to a junior high school out of our neighborhood as well. She is planning to be a doctor. A pediatrician. She has known what she wants to be when she grows up ever since we were eight. Me, I'm still thinking about it. There are so many things I love to do.

July 3, 1975 • Sherry and I take the bus up to Jamaica Avenue and go shopping for new clothes. Mommy gives us each $20 to pick out a new summer outfit. That's a lot of money.

We also go out to Long Island to visit different family friends. We go to Baldwin to visit our favorite babysitter and her family from when we were little. Gina used to come over and baby-sit us at night when Mommy and Daddy would have a dinner or dance to go to. Sherry and I loved it when she would come. She was really fun and pretty and nice, not mean like Yvette, another baby sitter used to be.

Gina and her sister, Lauren, talk to Sherry and me. I mean really talk. They ask us all about school and our friends and what we are going to do this summer. They show us their bedrooms and the cool clothes they actually know how to sew! They are grown and spend time with us. They jump double dutch and don't tease us about how we used to be double handed.

Lauren cornrows our hair. All over with beautiful beads. I love it and promise myself to try and keep it in for camp.

July 25, 1975 • For my birthday this year I have asked for this beautiful navy bag I saw in Gertz on the Avenue. It has yellow trim and enough space for me to pack all my summer outfits for weekend trips with our family. I love it so much and have been eyeing it for months.

Mommy takes me to pick out the bag. When I get home, I practice packing it. I will not take it to camp with me because I don't want it to get messed up. But I will take it on our next family outing. I can't wait! Maybe I can even carry my schoolbooks in it, once in a while.

Speaking of school, when I begin Ryan, I will be in class 7SP1. At the end of sixth grade when they assigned classes, it was decision-making time again. This time Mommy made the judgment call. Ryan has two-year year S.P. The S.P. stands for Special Progress. You have to have a high average to be accepted into the program. In the two-year S.P. program, the whole class studies an honors curriculum, completes seventh grade the first year, and then skips eighth grade and goes straight to ninth grade. Or you can take three-year S.P., which is honors courses without skipping a year.

I wanted to take three-year S.P. with Joyce and Annie. But Mommy decided it was better for me to skip a year because she thought it was a waste of time for me to be in junior high for three years when there is the opportunity to take an excelled program. So, I am in two-year S.P. Mommy says I can handle skipping a year. I hope so. Crystal will be there, but I will miss being with our other friends too.

September 5, 1975 • I can't believe summer went by so quickly. I remember when I was a little kid, summer seemed like it lasted forever. Camp Kaufman was great and we all definitely want to go back next year. I am going to invite even more of our friends to go next year. I think it would be so fun for us all to be together. School starts tomorrow. Junior High School. And I'm taking the bus there by myself. It's farther away than P.S. 131.

I got a new outfit for my first day. Unfortunately, it's still really hot and my outfit is for fall. I am going to wear it anyway.

September 18, 1975 • In the morning after riding the Q5AB, I transfer to the Special. That's the bus that takes us to Ryan from Jamaica Avenue. It is a city bus, but it goes directly to Ryan. No other stops. It's really crowded and loud. Kids pushing and shoving to get on, radios blasting. Even though the Special comes frequently, there are a lot of kids to take the bus. The bus driver keeps yelling, "Move to the back of the bus!" I get on and squeeze myself into a space in the middle of the bus. I hate being pushed to the back because all the kids smoke cigarettes and reefer in the back, even though it is only 8:15 in the morning. I hold my book bag close to me and watch my back.

Twenty minutes later, we arrive at Ryan. I jump off the bus in relief. Another morning of school has begun.

Ryan is a huge building that holds a lot of students. I have no idea how many. I just know there are about 14 classes on each grade. A lot of kids.

I race to homeroom. I am running late. As usual. Somehow, over the years I have gone from always being early like back in third grade when I used to walk to school with Alita and her mom, to always running late. How'd that happen?

Most of the kids are already in their seats. I rush to my wooden chair, sliding in just as the bell rings. I made it. Crystal and I look at each other and smile. It's time for the morning announcements.

Junior high is so different from elementary. I love walking from class to class. I like all the movement. Sometimes it's hard for me to sit still; I like to move, move, move. Lots of thoughts in my head and sometimes it gets boring sitting, sitting, sitting. So I like junior high.

I also like my classes. Well, most of them. Our social studies teacher is super strict. I think maybe he was in the Army. He almost makes one of my favorite subjects stink. Almost.

I am learning Spanish. And, I even have cooking. It's fun because we get to eat the food we cook, even if Mrs. Johnson does use one can of tuna to split up among the entire class when we are making macaroni salad.

At lunch time I still get to see Joyce and Annie, since all the seventh grade has lunch together.

There are lots of cute boys in this school, too. I notice them. But I don't say anything. I feel kind of shy and corny. I wouldn't know what to say to a guy I really liked. So, I leave flirting to the girls I see strolling down the hall, holding hands with their boyfriends or chasing or arguing with some boy they like. I have made lots of new friends though, boys and girls. I like junior high.

October 1, 1975 • There are always lots of fights on the Special. Our little group takes the Special together. We stay far away from the fighting crowd, as far away as it's possible to get, that is, on a bus.

When Crystal and I hang out together by ourselves, she pulls out her cigarettes. I guess she's been smoking for a while. I don't like cigarettes, but it's her choice to smoke and mine not to. We still have our easy relationship. Even though cigarettes aren't the only difference between us.

She tells me about her new boyfriend. She says he is really fine. He works near her mom's job in the city so she sees him when she goes there to visit her mom. She says he is Puerto Rican and his name is Jaime. He's 19. She says he loves her gray eyes and the way she kisses. Crystal tells me all about him. Even though I don't have a boyfriend or even know how to talk to guys. I mean really talk to them. I don't notice any guys that seem to like me. I wonder what ever happened to Christopher Corrin. I bet if I had stayed at P.S. 30, he might have become my boyfriend. I know that the year after I left, Alita started going with Stephan. And he was her Christopher when we used to joke and dream.

Oh, well. That's OK. Tonight Mommy, Sherry and I are going to see this new movie called *Black Girl* at the Rochdale Theater. I don't know what the second feature is, but I bet it will be good, too. And I am going to get my favorite movie treat, marshmallows.

November 3, 1975 • In gym we wear these ugly blue one-piece gym suits. The suit reminds me of what they call bloomers on TV. We had to stitch our names onto them in yellow thread. In gym we learn folk dances, have relay races and play basketball. In elementary school we had gym with the boys. Now we are separated and all the activities are with girls only. Why's that? I liked when we all, the boys and the girls, finally got to play punch ball together.

We just got this new boy in our class, Nick. He's black. Now there are four blacks in our class: me, Crystal, this guy Luther, who hardly says anything, he just waits for the bell to ring so he can hang out with his crew, and Nick. Nick is really cute! Even though he's only 12, he is super tall. Crystal and I both think he's really good looking. She says, "Let's wear cool outfits tomorrow." I go home and look at my wardrobe. I just don't have cool stuff like hers. I need cool new clothes. It's a good thing Christmas is coming up. The best I can do is my navy corduroy pants, navy turtleneck and yellowish gold vest. It looks OK. But I don't feel very good in it.

November 4, 1975 • Crystal struts in some tight jeans and this really funky purple shirt, with her pick in her back pocket. She says, "Hi," to Nick and starts flirting with him. I smile and stand behind her.

"So what's going on with you today, Sharon?" Nick asks. Oh, nothing, I say. Dumb answer. I just stand there and can't think of anything to add to that. Nick looks at me, smiles and then Crystal and Nick take off down the hall, laughing and talking.

I talk to another classmate, Rina. Hey, did you do the science homework? I ask. (How corny can you get?) I didn't, but I think I know how to do the problems, I joke with Rina. Inside, I am kicking myself. Why couldn't I think of something to say to Nick? God, I feel so tacky. We come into class laughing behind Nick and Crystal.

But since Nick's last name is Rogers, it is me he sits near in almost all of our classes.

November 21, 1975 • Even though I feel nervous around Nick, we've still gotten to be friends. He talks and laughs with Crystal, but he's always punching me on the arm and teasing me. I don't get it.

It's right before the Thanksgiving holiday. Our whole class is getting antsy because it is almost time for a break. We can't wait.

Today after school, a bunch of us went to the pizza shop to hang out. Joyce, Annie, Crystal, me, and a few other girls that live around Crystal's way. Nick came. When he comes, we all get kind of excited, but we play it off.

Sherry still walks down the hill from 131. These days she takes the bus with her friend Faith. Sometimes they come to the pizza shop, too. Sherry thinks Nick is OK but kind of doofey. She thinks Craig Ellis in her class is much cuter. Craig's cute, but he is so bad. He is funny, though. And even though he's two years younger than me, yes, OK, he is really cute, too.

But Nick, he's big and kind of mature. Well, sometimes, like when he's not punching my arm.

Now that we are in junior high, we hang out longer. Especially if it's a Friday. We girls all squeeze into one booth and Nick and his boy Jimmy—who we all think is really corny and boring because he wears high-water pants and is always saying, "That's cool, that's cool," several times, really fast—sit at the counter and swivel on their stools and joke with us. We make a slice or two of pizza last a very long time.

When we get home, Crystal and I call each other. Crystal likes to tease Nick. She says he's kind of corny himself. I laugh at her kidding, but I like Nick just the way he is. I just wish I could flirt with him like everybody else does.

I got my period. Actually I got it a few months ago. But I didn't tell anybody until it was over. I guess I had that feeling again of my body changing and feeling kind of private about it. I just used the sanitary napkins Mommy had given me to take to camp in case I got my period there. I was glad I didn't get it there. I remember this one girl in our unit, Claudia, got her period and she freaked out. Finally I confessed to Mommy that I got my period. She felt sad that I hadn't told her. I'm sorry Mommy, I just felt kind of self-conscious to tell you, and I just dealt with it myself. I feel terrible, depriving my mom of this moment of sharing. I promise myself that when there's another first, like having a baby when I am all grown up, I will let her know right away, so she'll feel great.

December 11, 1975 • My favorite book is *The Diary of Anne Frank*. It is this story about a young Jewish girl during the Holocaust. She and her family are in hiding from the Nazis in a secret annex. The whole time they are hiding, she is writing in her journal everything she thinks and experiences. She writes so beautifully, and sometimes when she talks about how she feels about growing up or tells her insights about people and life, I wish so desperately that I could talk with her because I think I know exactly what she means.

Anne is brave and courageous. Even when she does something dumb, she acknowledges it and is true to herself.

I try always to be true to myself, as well. I use Anne as a model. Even when Luther tries to get me to smoke a cigarette, I tell him no. And I don't care if he thinks I am corny. I guess people have their own version of what they believe in. I think about what it is I believe and then I try to live that way.

I guess Sherry and I pushed it last weekend, though.

Mommy and Daddy both smoke cigarettes. Sherry and I hate the smell. Especially now that I ride the Special. All that reefer and cigarette smoke drives me crazy. Last Saturday morning we took Mommy and Daddy's cigarettes and threw them out. We threw some down the building incinerator, flushed a few down the toilet and threw some out the window. I couldn't believe them; they made us retrieve the ones we threw out the window. They are even going to smoke cigarettes that fall two flights down and have been lying on the ground.

Christmas, 1975 • I know it sounds kind of silly, but in addition to all the cool new clothes I want to get for Christmas, I wish for Raggedy Ann. I realize I am a little old for her now, but I've always wanted her. So I put her on my Christmas list.

Each Christmas, there are so many gifts under the tree that they spread out across our living room! When I see the special box under the tree on Christmas morning, I am so excited. Then I open the box and pull out . . . Raggedy Andy.

I run into Mommy and Daddy's room and wake Mommy up. You got me Raggedy Andy, I say. I try hard not to sound ungrateful. "Oh my goodness," Mommy says. "We thought it was Raggedy Ann. Sherry and I looked all over for her. We'll take Andy back to the store and get you Ann."

No, I say. In this brief time, I've grown attached to Andy. I stare him in the eye and look at his smiling face. He can stay.

May 2, 1976 • Crystal dumped Jaime for Nick.

Our science teacher is Mr. Walsh. Science is an OK subject, pretty interesting. Mr. Walsh thinks he's funny when he's not. Yesterday I wore my favorite shirt, the turquoise bodysuit with the yellow flower in the center. Mr. Walsh actually came over with a watering can and said, "Oh, look a flower. Let's give it some water," and poured some water on me. Right on my hair! I couldn't believe it. Before I knew it, I'd grabbed the water bottle I had on my desk and threw some back on him. Got his shirt wet. Everybody was shocked and cracked up. There's that temper of mine flaring up. Mommy has told me to work on it. Mr. Walsh just kind of dabbed at his shirt with some paper towels and didn't even say anything. Maybe he knew he was wrong, too.

This summer we are going back to Camp Kaufman. I've succeeded in organizing a big gang of us to all go together. Besides me, Sherry, Toni and Joyce, even Crystal and Alita and a few other girlfriends are going.

Daddy has been promoted and is now the assistant director for the settlement house where he works. He has even longer hours now. When he is home, he sleeps a lot or else goes out. We don't take big family trips as we used to, either.

As we've gotten older, we don't want to go to the ball field anymore, get dirty, step in dog stuff and hang out in the hot sun. Eventually we started staying home. So did Mommy. But Daddy still goes. There are always double-headers and triple-headers on the weekends.

Still, the best part about the ball team is the trips.

Again, packing and traveling!

May 25, 1976 • Ever since we were little kids, on Memorial Day, July Fourth and Labor Day, the team has gone for playoffs somewhere in Pennsylvania, New Jersey or New York. We stay at Holiday Inns and Howard Johnsons. We love to swim and to play with the other kids from the team and to run around the motel and stay up late. All of the other teams we play are white. We are always the only black team there. Most of the time that is just fine. Once it was really uncomfortable.

For this Memorial Day trip, our parents let us invite Toni and Joyce. We are so excited. Pepper is coming, too, so it will be a full house. I hope Daddy won't do what happened last trip, when he went in to register; he came back out and said he forgot his wallet. I was so scared that we were going to have to drive back home and not be able to have our vacation. "Do you have any money?" he asked Mommy. Mommy paid for the trip.

Now that we are older, our parents let us go to the movies by ourselves. We hang out till late when we get back to the motel; Sherry and Toni keep talking about how cute that boy Craig is, in their class. I think he is going with two of their friends at the same time. We spend a lot of time trying to catch Pepper when he gets away and runs into the cornfields behind the motel.

Joyce and I talk about the fact that this September I will be in ninth grade and she will be in eighth, so we won't get to see each other as much at school. That part's a bummer. Still, we have the whole summer to have a great time.

I practice my cornrowing. I have been doing it ever since I taught myself after Loren did my hair. I am getting to be really good. Sometimes Sherry still lets me do her hair for her.

August 15, 1976 • Another great weekend. Sunday, Sherry and I spent the whole day in our pajamas, watching all these great old movies on television. Old classics that Mommy has reminisced about over the years, telling us the stories of how her grand-mother would take her and Uncle Louchy to the movies for Saturday matinees.

So, Sherry and I finally got to see *The Glass Menagerie*. It was excellent, as well as being quite bittersweet. Then we watched *It's a Mad Mad Mad Mad World* (or however many "mads" there are in the title). It was hilarious, and Sherry and I have plenty of silly repertoire to last us for the next few weeks. We are sure to drive Mommy crazy.

September 8, 1976 • Ninth grade. We've skipped a year. We are 9SP1. All of a sudden we are the youngest people on the grade. Most of the time that's OK because our whole class is together. At lunchtime, though, I don't know any of the people, except for my class. I miss lunchtime with the eighth graders. I wish I were there. Get used to it, Sharon, this is your new grade, I remind myself. You and your whole class are now ninth graders. This is your last year in junior high. Then it's on to high school.

October 15, 1976 • A few years ago our family joined a family club called Hansel and Gretal. Every month we do different activities with the other kids in our age group. There are also activities for everyone as a family and stuff for the parents to do, as well.

Hansel and Gretal is OK. Sometimes we do really fun things like going ice-skating at Rockefeller Center and to plays.

Some of the kids are really nice, but I find some of them pretty snotty, not to mention wannabes. Honestly, some of the parents are, too. I don't like it when people act that way. Adults or kids. Sometimes Hansel and Gretal does things that I find really inane, like the time they actually planned an etiquette session. I found the perspective of the parents who were planning it a turnoff. Some of them remind me of those stage moms you see on TV, complete with the airs and attitude to go with it. Mommy taught me how to set a table and what forks to use when I was a little kid. I told Mommy that is not how I want to spend my time. I chose not to go to the session. I was happy she let me make my own choice. Mommy says the whole experience is good exposure. Hmm.

December 2, 1976 • Last night I was thinking about the word happiness. Sherry and I often discuss different aspects of life. We'll ask each other, "Do you understand the concept of . . ." whatever it is we want to talk about. That's our favorite phrase.

I realize it's been a while since I wrote a poem. After thinking long and hard I wrote this one today when I got home from school:

LIFE IS A SONG

Life is a song
Which we all sing
Some of us do not know all the words
Others sing with such harmony
That we look on in amazement and envy
In life we learn many verses
Some tunes we find impossible to carry
When the song comes to an end
The music is forever lost
And the lyrics begin anew
The vocalist is laid to rest
Life continues on
One long, beautiful, painful song.

January 26, 1977 • Our crew at school doesn't bother to take the Special anymore. We have found a way to remove ourselves from that negative situation and take a more positive way home.

We walk over two blocks and catch the regular city bus. Have our own good time.

Jimmy, Nick's friend who is still boring, writes me a note. He is getting ready to move with his family to Arizona.

In it, he tells me that he liked me and that he had hoped we could go together but that I never responded to him. (He didn't put it that way but it's essentially what he meant.) Actually, he said he thought we could be tight. Then he put an asterisk next to tight and wrote at the bottom of the page, "Tight means close." Does he think I am so not down that I don't know that? I guess he does. Crystal and I thought that part was really funny. I don't like Jimmy, though, for more than a friend. To be honest, not even particularly as a friend. Oh well, I got out of that one since he's moving.

This is not my idea of romance. Not even close to the way Harlequin guys woo their girls. Or how I'd like to be wooed.

I wish Jimmy good luck on his move. He says, "Thanks." He seems kind of mad at me.

January 28, 1977 • Mommy has decided to go back to school. Sherry and I think that is great. She has her college degree from Fordham and a master's, but now she is going to return and study some new educational curriculum. She also will take a course that she can use if she were to go to law school. I guess that's always been a dream of hers.

Mommy and Daddy are arguing. Again. Daddy doesn't want Mommy to go to school. Sherry and I can hear them through the wall by Sherry's bed. He keeps telling her she doesn't need to go. She keeps explaining to him why she wants to go.

Finally Sherry and I go to bed. We don't even go in and say good night as we usually do. We just go to sleep, rather disgusted. I wake up in the middle of the night to go to the bathroom. It must be about two o'clock in the morning. I walk by Mommy and Daddy's bedroom on the way to the bathroom. I can't believe it; they are still up, having the same conversation. Mommy's class is tomorrow morning. To take the train to get to Hoffstra, she has to leave by 7A.M.

Why are you still talking about this? I ask them. Daddy doesn't bother to answer me. Why don't you just go to bed so you can get up and go to class tomorrow? I say to Mommy. Right in front of Daddy.

What Daddy is saying doesn't make sense to me, I think in my head, Why shouldn't Mommy take this opportunity? Isn't that what he encourages and helps the people at his center to do? Why is Mommy any different? He's not home anyway, and Sherry and I can take care of ourselves on a Saturday morning or a Tuesday evening. We are very independent.

"Maybe you're right," Mommy says in response to my question.

Good night, I say.

When Sherry and I wake up the next morning, Mommy has left for school. Daddy wakes up about noon.

"Where's Mommy?" he asks. "She's at school," we say, matter-of-factly. He looks angry.

February 9, 1977 • Oh, man. Hansel and Gretal has scheduled a dance. A real dance. I've never been to one. Most of my friends have. Sherry and I practice dances in our bedroom. But I sure don't actually want to do them in front of people. I'm not ready. I want to be a kid a while longer. Not a young woman like they keep calling me.

I'm not going, I decide! Suddenly, I feel better.

February 12, 1977 • The night of the dance. I know this dance will forever be in my mind as "the-make-you-or-break-you dance."

That is what Mommy and Daddy say it is. I think that's dumb. How can one dance do that? Still this time, it is Mommy and Daddy forcing me to go. They say I'll be just totally not accepted if I don't go. I don't care. Who ever heard of a kid not wanting to go to a dance and the parents making them go? That's funny; it is so totally the opposite of what I read in books about teenagers. It's similar to when I am lying in my bed reading a Harlequin and Mommy comes in the room. I shove the Harlequin under my pillow and pretend to be watching TV. Innocently hurting my eyes, especially since I already wear glasses. Most parents would rather see their kids reading than watching television.

It's not that Mommy doesn't know I read them, but she says, "Put those books away, Sharon, they are not real life."

But back to the dance. They're making me go. This is one of those times when Sherry is lucky she is two years younger than I. She gets to stay home. Lucky stiff.

The dance is in the Watsons' basement. That's right, Valerie Watson is in Hansel and Gretal, too.

It's dark down there and the music is blaring. Lots of folks are on the little dance floor, dancing. I slide over to the wall and find a spot to stand. It's as horribly uncomfortable as I thought it would be. I know the dance they are doing, the Uptown. I practiced it at home with Sherry. But I'm not about to try it tonight. Besides, nobody is asking me to dance anyway.

Halfway through the night, it gets worse. Valerie Watson says, "Sharon, are you going to hold the wall up all night?"

Valerie, I say, I'd appreciate it if you'd keep your comments to yourself.

She looks surprised. I stare straight ahead, glad the night is almost over. It's not that I want to be out on the dance floor. I don't. It's just that I'd rather be doing the things that make me happy right now. When I'm ready to dance, I'll dance.

February 15, 1977 • I was mad about what Valerie said to me, but I've been thinking about it, too. I am me. I'm not anybody else. If I don't dance all night, I don't dance all night. And I can't let Valerie make me feel bad about it. Or anybody else. Not even Mommy and Daddy. I have to believe that if I hadn't gone to that dance, I would still be me. And that would be OK. Even if they think it is a make-it-or-break-it opportunity, I don't have to see it that way.

Maybe they can make me go to the dance. But that doesn't mean I have to agree with their philosophy. I have my own way of looking at life. Some of it's like theirs and some of it's not. And even if it feels like I'm weird sometimes, I don't really want to be like Valerie or even Crystal. I just want to be me. But I do want to be the best me that I can be. Sometimes, that's the hardest part.

March 1, 1977 • We are having orientation for high school! It's really time. I am going to Jamaica High School. Some of my old friends from 131, like Joyce and Tracy, are going to different high schools throughout the city like Music and Art or Bronx High School of Science. I'll miss them.

Crystal, Nick and a bunch of us will be at Jamaica together. We are all pretty excited. Inside, I'm nervous, too. I hope high school is a place where I have more space to do my own thing, now that I am figuring out more of what that is.

Pack Originality

SOMETIMES, IT'S A MATTER OF DARING TO BE YOURSELF.
I say daring, because it can be easier said than done.

When I look back over those adolescent years, just being myself, learning myself, expressing myself . . . amidst a world of contrasting messages . . . was a major undertaking.

I believe to Pack Originality is to be your own, unique person.

Honing a sense of self and allowing one's character to develop without stunting it for fear of being different.

It's imagination, individuality, authenticity . . . Originality.

In identifying the Originality of each of us, it's an opportunity to celebrate and respect it in each other.

And so, as a girl, budding into young womanhood, I found the chance to discover myself, instead of trying to discover how to be like everybody else. And to allow myself the freedom to be Sharon, learn her and develop her. Even when I liked her and when I didn't. Not to give up on myself or want to trade me in. Because Sharon is what God has given me to work with.

I've learned, you've only got one you. I am thankful that I understood this early. One spirit. One heart. One body. One mind. So I've come to learn, and it's been a "long journey home," that you are whatever you make you, with whatever you've got. I believe the trick is to appreciate this and evolve ever higher, holding onto the hand of the girl you once were, while extending the other hand to the woman you'll be tomorrow, linked together as one you, yet always growing.

3

Coming of Age in an Unromantic World

October 13, 1977 • "Yo, baby! Can I come with you?" I hear from behind me. And a bunch of other stuff. Guys always yell stuff at us. As we walk up the hill, there are always lots of home-boys trying to get a rap. There is another high school right behind ours that until recently was an all-boys school. I have gotten kind of used to it. But it still gets on my nerves. Especially when they get mad if you don't answer.

The guy yelling at me just now has all this gold around his neck and a gold tooth with his initial on it. He follows me all the way up the hill. Trying to rap the whole time.

"Yo, where you from?" he asks me. Here, I assure him. "You sound like you from another country," he says. "You don't talk like you from around here."

I feel kind of bad when he says that. I am tired of hearing it.

Finally, at the entrance to Jamaica, when he hasn't succeeded in getting my phone number, he switches course and starts yelling at me, "You wasn't that fine, anyway." That makes me laugh, but I keep it to myself. I'm not crazy, and I don't want to get this guy any more pissed off than he already is.

Jamaica High School is so huge. It has multilevels, and there are kids from junior high schools all over Queens. The sophomores alone are about 870 kids.

The building is a rather stately stone structure with lots of green grass lining the fringe of the property. Students hang out all over the grounds and in front of the building. We have a spot where our crew likes to congregate when we get to school. I hardly ever make it there, though. I am always rushing to get to first period.

October 28, 1977 • I joined the Model Congress at school. In Model Congress we reenact the interaction of the Senate and the House, working to get bills passed. I'm finding this process so in-triguing, and I love lobbying. It's a chance to speak in a forum where the whole process is speaking out for what you believe in . . . creating a way of sharing your concerns and opinions so that you can enroll others in your beliefs.

I am sponsor for a "bill" and am leading my committee in the fight to get it passed. I will be representing Jamaica High at the Model Congress at CUNY Queens College. And later this winter we're taking a trip to Washington, D.C., to observe the real process in action. I can't wait. I guess there's a lot I can't wait for.

I'm enjoying tenth grade. I'm relieved, because, deep down inside, I was nervous about whether I'd like it or not. Really, like whether I'd feel I could fit in. There's lots of life I am wondering about still, but at least I know I've found some things here that are for me. Sherry likes Ryan Junior High, too. She has some of my old teachers, including Mr. Crow for social studies. All the kids say he is still running boot camp.

November 2, 1977 • Now that I am fourteen and a teenager and Sherry is almost a teenager, Mommy is letting us redecorate our bedroom. The three of us have been spending some wonderful weekends, visiting furniture stores and reading magazines and designing our bedroom.

Today we found these great beds that are in the shape of an L. On the short part of the L, the bed slides under this table that has a green bolster on it so it can become a lounging chair, and the other bed has bolsters on it as well, so that it is like a couch. This is only the beginning! Even though our money is still pretty tight, Mommy is managing to work miracles so that we can redo our room.

November 4, 1977 • Nick is in my homeroom. We still sit right near each other. And he still teases me a lot. We have several of our classes together, too. One of them is geometry. I'm having a hard time with it. Sometimes, it just doesn't make sense to me. All this proving theorems. Maybe if I spent more time working on my geometry, I'd get it more, but it just doesn't interest me.

Today in class, I am so proud because for my homework I proved my theorem and feel confident of the answer. I volunteer to prove it on the board in front of the class.

I'm standing in front of the class, and the teacher is pointing out that one of my assumptions is incorrect. Now it changes all of the other assumptions I have established. She is waiting for me to fix it. I don't see how I can change it to make it come out right.

What if you draw the line from here to here? I ask. "No, that's not going to work," she says. She looks at me expectantly, waiting for another suggestion. I have none. I stand there in agony. I wish she would let me go sit down. I look out at my classmates' faces. Nick is laughing so hard, his face is red.

I'm still standing here, and the teacher is making me think of ways to fix it. None of them work. Finally the bell rings.

My head held low, I slink to my seat to get my books. Nick is still cracking up. I am so embarrassed and feel so bad that I sit down at my desk and start crying. Right in class.

Nick stays with me and tells me it will be OK. Even though I still feel really stupid, having him pat me on the shoulder, instead of laughing, helps.

I have to hurry or I'll be late for my next class.

December 15, 1977 • I've been wearing glasses since elementary school. First just for reading and then all the time. I never cared before. But now, even with my cool new glasses, I hate wearing them.

They make me look tacky.

January 13, 1978 • I have this insatiable curiosity to know what happened to Anne Frank and her family after they were caught. I go to the school library and pore over other books about her and her family and what little is known about them in the concentration camps. I hang on to small tidbits of information about her. She lived three days or so after her sister died. And I think about how that must have felt. Only Anne's father survived to share her story. Again, I wish I could have known Anne. Except I do, through her diary.

My journal has become my close friend, as well. In it I continue to write my most secret emotions and feelings, the ones that are sometimes difficult to admit even to myself.

DEAR LOVE,
I waited for you
Day after day
To come to me
To turn a street corner
Or just trip over my books
As I sat there, dreaming, about you
But you never came

As I sat there
Waiting
And day after day
Everyone walked right by me
As I sat there
Waiting
For you
And still you didn't come
So I told myself
He'll be here
Give him time
He's out there
Somewhere
Looking for you too
Until, just now, when I realized
that maybe you aren't coming
Because you're not there
Are you
a figment of my imagination
Just a particle
of my impossible dream?

June 1, 1978 • Life at home is kind of weird these days.

Most of the time, Sherry and I talk to Daddy only on the phone when he calls from work. Even though he gets home from work in time to walk Pepper for his night walk at 11:00 P.M., he still makes Sherry and me do it. We have tried to talk to him about it because we don't feel safe walking Pepper by ourselves out that late. We've been doing it for the past few years. We have to walk Pepper down the back steps to sneak him outside, since you're not allowed to have dogs here. We can't take the elevator with him. The back stairs are the least safe, but that's the way we have to go. We have heard stories of people being jumped or attacked in the stairway, even adults. After one particularly scary-sounding incident, we even stuck a hammer under my coat, for protection.

Daddy doesn't listen. "Just walk the damn dog," he says.

October 23, 1978 • Crystal has set me up with a blind date. Her boyfriend, Dazzlin Devon, is a DJ who goes to Jamaica, too. She and Nick dropped each other a while ago. Dazzlin doesn't always come to school, though. Sometimes Crystal takes the day off to be with him. But she always gets her work done.

I am really nervous. Crystal and I don't talk about it, but we both know I haven't dated anybody. I and another friend of mine, Clare, who hasn't had a date either, talk about it all the time. We've even formed our own club, she, Sherry, and I: the C.I.A.—cute-intelligent-accursed . . . with the emphasis on "accursed" and a question mark on "cute."

Mommy spends a lot of time talking to me about my feelings about myself. I am glad that I can confide in her, that she is my friend. Mommy always tells me I'm pretty. But I don't feel pretty or cool or anything. I guess deep down inside, I feel kind of bad about myself when it comes to guys. If I am so pretty, how come no guys like me? Mommy says I have to give it a chance. That I just can't see it. "All the guys like you," she says. Yeah, right, I say. They like girls like Crystal. Girls that they can enjoy hanging out with. Who aren't shy with them and know what to say. Who like to talk, or flirt, or fool around.

Don't get me wrong. I love my friend Crystal. Over the years, I've just come to think of us as different.

October 28, 1978 • The movie is a horror film. Why'd it have to be that? I get so scared at horror movies. I always have bad dreams afterward. One time Sherry and I went to see *Dawn of the*

Dead, and I begged her to hold my hand walking back home, although it was broad daylight. I was so scared; even though she thought it was dumb, she held my hand.

Crystal wasn't exaggerating. My date, Lawrence, is really fine. I can't think of anything to say the whole time. I sit through the movie, stiff in my seat. Really, I am so petrified of the film, I can't move. I wish I could hide my face in his shoulder. But I am too scared to do that, too. The other kind of scared. He looks kind of bored. Is it me, the movie or both?

We come out of the theater, and as we stand in a group, I catch sight of my reflection. I got my first hair relaxer three months ago. I think it must have been too strong because my hair is falling out. In the mirror, it looks so thin, it looks see-through. Oh God, I feel so embarrassed and inept.

Devon and Lawrence say bye and go to catch their bus. Crystal and I walk slowly toward the bus terminal. I know I won't be seeing Lawrence again.

Thanks, Crys, I really appreciate the hookup. "Sure," Crystal says. Crystal, never one to criticize me, doesn't talk about how lame I was. Crystal is a true friend.

December 5, 1978 • Sitting in my favorite class. Humanities. It's an extra honors class that combines social studies, English, art and literature. It brings together all my favorite subjects from over the years. I love it. We learn all about the impressionists and other art time periods. And have the opportunity to visit many museums and exhibits throughout the city. I've got lots of great friends in the class, and since it is two periods long, we get really comfortable as we all study and talk.

We read the classics and have heated discussions about what the authors really meant. Sometimes I think it is silly the way Mr. Masters talks about all the things the author intended when he wrote a paragraph. Couldn't it just be that we make it mean what we think it means, not what the author intended? We spend a lot of time on *Ordinary People*. I love reading *Catcher in the Rye*. It's all about this boy, Holden Caufield. Even though he is really wacky, I admire that he has a very different perspective on life. On my own I've been reading books by lots of different poets and writers. They inspire me in my poetry, and I've gone from performing *Fiddler on the Roof*, like when we were little kids, to acting out songs and performing and interpreting poetry in front of Sherry, Crystal and Mommy and whoever else will listen and not laugh.

December 10, 1978 • I can't believe we are almost through our first semester of junior year.

Nick, as usual, is in most of my classes. But so is his best friend, Hugo. I've decided my crush on Hugo is way bigger than my crush on Nick!

Usually after school, we all hang out at the good ol' pizza shop. Or else we go to get beef patties and cocoa bread next door. Flaky with lots of spiced meat inside, their smell wafts to us before we even squeeze in the door. Squeeze in, cause it's always packed. Everybody knows the deal on how good those patties are.

Crystal's big brother Winston even comes. We've all been in school together the past few years; we finally caught up to him. Winston is really quiet. He goes with another friend of ours, Holly. They spend most of their time at Winston's house, since Crys and Winston's grandmother works long hours. Crys and her mom still don't get along. But now Crys just doesn't sweat it. Sometimes, she even stays over at my house on weekends. Sometimes she stays at Devon's because his mom doesn't care; she's got other things on her mind.

Soon it's going to be time to take the SATs. College preparation. I can't believe college is coming up. It seems like just yesterday I was singing "Billy, Don't Be a Hero." Now I'm singing that new jam, "Ain't No Stoppin Us Now," and getting ready for college. We are taking the PSATs now, and we'll take the SATs next year. I don't mind tests too much. I hope I do really well. I want to go away to college. I think that would be a lot more exciting than taking the train to school and living at home. I want the whole college experience I have always dreamt about.

I have come to the conclusion that whatever is going on in life, it is so important to keep dreaming and believe that there is lots of good stuff ahead. Even when, sometimes, things feel bad.

A DREAM

The worst thing that can happen to a person in this inverse world
is to be without a dream.
A dream is something to look forward to,
To hold on to when you feel empty or without hope.
A dream is something to aim for.
It gives you a purpose,
A reason for living.
A dream is something you own,
That's just yours
To share with yourself, in secret moments,
While the world continues to revolve around you,
To look at, and think about, just for the joy of knowing it's there
Secret and apart from everyday life,
And yet in there, inside you all the time,
Waiting to be fulfilled
A dream is something happy, a promise that might never be kept
And yet is always there
To hope, and wish for
A dream is something that,
When broken,

Must be rebuilt
Or you will be no one
You're nothing . . .
Without
A Dream.

December 12, 1978 • I'm now singing with the Jamaica High School Chorus. I love it. We even have robes. I've also chosen to quit the piano lessons I've been taking for years. Sherry's elected to continue. Even though we come from a family of piano players, I just don't feel it is my strong suit. Besides, I never practice. I figured it was time to spare my piano teacher. But I love to sing.

In chorus, we sing lots of beautiful songs and have a great time entertaining audiences. None of my buddies are in chorus, but I have met some wonderful new friends there, especially Justine. She is a year behind me and lives in Flushing. She lives with her older sister Sharise, and she never talks about her mom or dad. We are both in the alto section together. We sing "Hark How the Bells" for Christmas time. The altos get the boring part that goes "Ding dong ding dong" over and over again.

This year I also have physics. Now, there's a challenging subject. While I love my humanities classes, my Spanish class and some of the great electives I've been able to snag, like this experimental psychology class, I don't like physics. And it shows.

January, 5, 1979 • Sherry and I stay up late every night to watch this crazy show, *Mary Hartman, Mary Hartman*. Mommy thinks it's absurd, but Sherry and I think it is hysterical. Especially the episode where Tom gets stabbed in the back by a Christmas tree.

Our crew has started going to the Y to swim on Friday evenings. Nick, Hugo, Crystal, Devon, even Winston and Holly go, too. Sherry and I look forward to it as our fun night out. Justine has started coming, also. The parents drive us there in the evening, drop us off, and then one or two of them car pool to pick us up. After we swim, we go to McDonald's to eat. We have such a good time all swimming together. Most all of us are pretty good swimmers, so we play, dive, have contests, and tease and mess with each other.

April 25, 1979 • The past few weeks I've been so preoccupied thinking about the national NAACP ACT-SO dramatics competition in Louisville, Kentucky. I won the Elmhurst competition—so now I have qualified for the national finals. I am going to perform an excerpt from Ntozake Shange's *for colored girls who have considered suicide when the rainbow is enuf.*

I love acting and Ntozake's poetry. It's so wonderful to perform her work, which is all poetry and beauty and raw life . . . to my ears. At home, Mommy and I have spent hours each week rehearsing together, acting out the joys and pains of my character as I share insights on being a loving colored girl in a bittersweet society.

Everywhere I go, I am reciting in my head the section from *No More Love Poems,* "Ever since I realized there waz someone callt a colored girl, an evil woman, a bitch or a nag, I have been tryin not to be that and leave bitterness in somebody else's cup."

My dramatics coach, Simon, from the neighborhood theater near our house, is very encouraging. "Excellent!" he shouts when I do a particularly fine enactment. "Now do it again."

April 26, 1979 • Evan Marshall is our old neighbor. He and his family, the Marshall family, used to live in the back section of our building. When I was really little, I used to go to the Marshalls' house in the morning to walk to kindergarten. Terri, the daughter, is the same age as me. Mrs. Marshall was always really nice. She used to buy the best tasting bread. Sherry and I called it circle bread (because it was shaped like a circle instead of square like Wonder Bread). We got Mommy to start buying it for our house. Terri's two big brothers, Evan and Lee, would tease Terri and me unmercifully. Deep down inside, I loved it because that's when they paid attention to us. It felt good to have big brothers. Even if it was just for brief moments. Terri was good in all sports and popular outside with the kids in our building. The times when Sherry and I did go out to play, Terri always used to watch out for us and make sure (as Mommy would say) nobody got too smart with us. (They used to get pretty "smart" sometimes.) All the kids respected Terri, plus she had two big brothers. I always wished I had a big brother to watch out for me. Now I wish I had a big brother so that maybe I could date his friends. But I hear from my friends with brothers, that's not at all the way it works.

Anyway, back to the present. Evan attends Cornell University in upstate New York. The whole family moved out to Long Island several years ago, but our families kept in touch.

Earlier this year, Evan came and visited. He spent several hours telling me all about Cornell, answering every question I had about college, regardless of whether the question was convoluted, minute, or brilliant and insightful. He took the time and answered them all. Evan was also cute and smart and nice. I really appreciated the time he took to tell me about school. It was the first time in my life I ever had that detailed a conversation about what college is really like, with somebody who is actually there living it.

He invited me and our family up to visit Cornell and experience it for ourselves. I have been excited about going for months. Mommy and Sherry are pretty excited, too. Daddy promised we'd go this spring. We need to select the dates so we can let Evan know. His school year will be winding down really soon.

April 28, 1979 • It's Saturday early afternoon, and I have waited to catch Daddy awake and at home.

When is a good date for the family to go visit Evan Marshall at Cornell? I ask Daddy. He's standing at the kitchen windows and Mommy is cooking at the stove.

"We're not going," Daddy replies. I can't believe he just said that. Why not? I ask, shocked.

"We're not going all the way up there," Daddy says.

It's only about a five-hour drive, Daddy. We've been planning this for so long, I say. Daddy doesn't respond. I just don't understand. What is the problem with going? I persist.

"No," from Daddy.

This isn't fair. I don't get it, I state in disgust.

I see the beloved trip fading away in my mind's eye.

"Go to hell, Sharon," Daddy says.

I walk out of the room. Dry-eyed. I leave Daddy's presence. And I know I am leaving something behind me in that room. Something that I can't regain.

May 7, 1979 • I wrote this one for humanities. They asked us to write how we define happiness. I decided to write mine as prose.

HAPPINESS

Happiness means many different things to many different people.
There is no definition of happiness;
It is an indefinable word
It is a feeling that we each have deep inside
Which we get at times and try to hold onto.
Happiness can be elusive, sliding away just when we think
We have it securely in our grasp.
Happiness is an emotion we all experience
Some of us constantly, others once in a lifetime

Happiness is a goal we try to achieve
And though it may come only once
It is something to always appreciate and remember.

June 2, 1979 • I can't believe it. Finally, it happened. Today I was sitting on the Q5AB on my way home from school, and I met this guy Mario. He started talking to me on the bus ride. Kind of flirting. And I found myself able to flirt back. Maybe it helped that I felt great in my gray corduroy Jordaches.

He got off at my stop, and we hung out and talked in front of my building for a long time. We talked and laughed and smiled a lot. "I like those pants," he said. To tell you the truth, I can't remember what else we talked about, even though it only happened about ten minutes ago. He said he'd walk me to my apartment. We got off the elevator at my floor, and I stopped there and said, Hey, it was really nice meeting you. "Yeah, you too," he said. And then he leaned over and kissed me. A light kiss good-bye.

A kiss.

June 13, 1979 • I'm here in Louisville. Finally, time for the NAACP competition. There are guys and girls here from all over the country. Even from California, where I've never been, but which sounds like such a cool place. Dick Gregory, a famous activist and writer, spoke at the national dinner we had. The people in our Queens group are really great and I've made some new friends, like Denine. The guys are really nice, too, especially David. We've been having some really cool conversations. Even though I doubt I'll see him after this trip, God, does it feel good to be able to really connect with a guy.

My throat has been hurting me all day. My voice is starting to sound more and more scratchy, and the competition is only two days away.

June 14, 1979 • My throat hurts even worse! I can barely talk. Denine keeps making me cups of tea. David went to the store to get me some cough medicine, but nothing helps.

Mr. Lester says he is going to take me to the hospital here in Louisville. I am worried.

June 15, 1979 • I have strep throat. That's what the doctor says. It is very difficult to even understand my voice when I speak.

June 16, 1979 • Our whole team walks over to the competition site, a huge auditorium with thousands of people. The competition will be broadcast on television. I think long and hard about how I've worked. How much I, my coach Simon, and Mommy have put into this. I think about Ntozake Shange's beautiful poem, still dancing in my head. I am going to do it.

"Sharon Simpson," the announcer says into the microphone. I walk onto the stage in my yellow leotard and flowing skirt, a print scarf on my head, and begin.

I'm talking pretty fast . . . too fast. . . .

I soften my voice lovingly on the part where I try so desperately to share with my man what is honestly in my heart. I listen to my voice intone,

Niggah—get outta here wit alla that. I didn't have any of that for you. I brought you what joy I found and I found joy. Honest fingers round my face . . .

It's not coming out the way I rehearsed, because you can barely understand my words, my voice is so hoarse and muffled. But I just keep going, the audience hushed as I longingly whisper my colored girl's final avowal.

I finish. I hear applause. I walk off the stage.

It is the hardest thing I have ever done. And I did it!

I don't win. I doubt most people even know what I said. But

I did it! I feel so powerful and have such a sense of . . . what is it? Accomplishment. Yes. I will never forget this moment.

July 10, 1979 • It's amazing how fast time is flying. Summer vacation, already. I have been working in the summer since I turned fourteen and got my working papers. Mostly tutoring jobs and camp. This summer I have a job as a camp counselor at a church camp right near Hillcrest High School, the school Sherry will attend in the fall. That's right, Sherry starting high school. I can't believe it. She has chosen Hillcrest instead of Jamaica because they have a medical program to which she has been admitted. Most all of her crew is going to Jamaica, but Sherry knows what she wants. She has always had incredible determination and focus. I admire her. Hillcrest is actually only about a ten-minute walk from Jamaica, so we'll still get to hang out together a lot.

Sherry's premed program is the same one Alita is in. Even though we are still in the same Senior Girl Scout troop, we've drifted apart otherwise. It really hurt for a while. It's fine now, though. We both have our own crews we hang with at school.

I've gotten my hair in braids for the summer. Often I do it myself, but this time I went to the beauty parlor. They wove in beads and hair extensions for a really intricate design. Hardly anybody wears their hair like this, and my friends haven't decided if they like it yet. But I love it, and I am teaching myself how to do it, experimenting on one braid in the back of my head. I think I must have been a hair stylist in another life.

July 12, 1979 • At camp I love working with the kids. I guess in part that's because even though I will be turning 16 later this month, I remember what it feels like to be a little kid. And I remember my promise to myself. When I was little, I vowed to treat children with respect, love, and dignity. And to expect that in return. Now's the time to put that in motion.

My unit is run by a senior counselor; a man named Don. The junior counselors are this fine (and I do mean fine, except he is about the same height as me, 5′4″) guy Oscar, and me.

The children have all the typical camping activities, so it's a pretty decent agenda for them: arts and crafts, swimming, field, trips, snacks, lunch, playtime, etc. Not like the tutoring camp last year where I worked, when we had to invent everything to create fun experiences for the kids, since we had no supplies, pool, or anything. Here, most all of the activities take place in a pretty small space on the campgrounds. Then we take the children to the park nearby.

I like Oscar; we get along pretty well. Sometimes Oscar comes in with these long scratches on his chest. "My girlfriend, Marisa," Oscar explains with a laugh. Wow, I'm thinking, that must have been one hot night. I can't even imagine it. For me, I am still dreaming of the day that a guy will really want to go with me, and I with him. That's what I want. Sleeping together, actually doing it, seems light-years away. Like when I get married. My only frame of reference are my Harlequins, Crystal's stories and my good-bye kiss from Mario, whom I never bumped into again.

There's this one little boy in our unit, Oscar calls Fat Jefferson. I tell Oscar I don't think that's a nice thing to call him, but he just laughs and says, "Fat Jefferson, get your a—— over here."

The kids are really fun and sweet. I love talking to them and sharing with them about life . . . and encouraging them. Especially to be good to each other. And that it's OK to be yourself. The kids love Oscar and me. They are always teasing us and asking us if we go together. The kids have also pointed out that I have really small teeth. They say mine are the same size as theirs. Actually, I guess they are right.

August 1, 1979 • Today Jefferson was really acting up. Messing with the other kids. I sat down to talk with him. I didn't yell at him, I just really talked to him with love and respect. And I let him know I wouldn't take any less than that from him. It was great, because after a few minutes he truly started to talk back. And I listened.

It worked! He stopped acting up and came back over to the group and was cool with the kids and with me.

This was the best day.

August 23, 1979 • This summer we've been really low on money. Since Mommy is a teacher, she gets a check at the beginning of the summer to tide us over until September. Sherry is baby-sitting. We pool all of our funds. (I still buy some cool summer outfits too, I admit.)

This weekend Daddy took the last $10 and walked over to Off Track Betting, more commonly known as OTB. He wouldn't listen to anyone's protests on the subject. I don't know how he thought he was going to turn that $10 into more money. He seems to think OTB is the answer. I sure don't. Sherry and I made penny rolls from Grandmother Thompson's old penny bottles. I will take them to the bank after work tomorrow.

September 8, 1979 • Everybody is talking about the fact that this is our last year in high school. Then it will be time to go out into the world. I have been thinking about my life a lot lately. I have to write all sorts of essays for my college applications. Essays on what my philosophy is toward life, what experiences taught me a valuable lesson and deep stuff like that.

I think Sherry and I learned early that the world is a huge and diverse and exciting place. Our world was big pretty quickly. I know our parents raised us that way intentionally so we wouldn't have a narrow view of the world or the people that inhabit it.

Thinking back, I see how frequently Mommy and Daddy took us to all sorts of places, especially having to do with their jobs, as a teacher and a social worker, so that we saw how lots of different folks experienced life.

Random events flash through my mind. Like back when Mommy used to teach at Junior High School 8. There was a car theft ring at the school. She made the mistake of parking her car in front of the school building, only to discover it stolen.

"Oh, Mrs. Simpson," her students said pityingly, "why'd you park it there? You know that's where the cars get stolen from."

"I was in a rush to get into work," she said. "But I must pick up my girls," my mother went on determinedly. She put the word out that she had to pick up her two little girls after school and asked some of her students to relay this message. Lo and behold, the Chevrolet Malibu was back that afternoon. The lock was gone from the passenger door, but the car ran, and she picked us up. None of the other cars were ever found.

Or the time Pepper was choking on the steak bone Daddy gave him. Sherry saved Pepper by standing him on his hind legs and executing the Heimlich maneuver she'd recently learned in school. My wonderful sister, ever resourceful, really saved the day on that one. Daddy was standing there saying, "Oh, Pep's a goner." I was screaming, Help! Mommy was in shock. And Sherry saved him.

These memories stick with me. Flashes of memory that echo in my mind. I believe they make such a lasting impression upon us, and who we are. The lessons our parents teach us stick, the valuable strong ones and the ones we do our best to unlearn.

Sherry and I talk a lot about home. Things have changed so much over the years. We aren't sure why. But it has gotten to the point that we are glad Daddy comes home very late most every night. I finally confess to Sherry that when I hear Daddy's key turning in the door, my stomach tightens up in knots. She tells me she feels the same way. Why does Daddy seem so mean and uncaring? we ask each other. But we don't have any answers.

I tell Sherry about a time recently, when we fell asleep in bed with Mommy one night while watching late-night TV. Since we were in Daddy's spot, he slept in my bed. The next day when I came home from school, I discovered that he had spilled a cup of coffee on and behind my bolster, on my covers and down the side of my bed.

He just left it there, I tell Sherry. He didn't even clean it up.

We talk about Mommy and Daddy's relationship. It doesn't seem like there is one to us. Why does Mommy stay with him and take this kind of treatment? we ask each other. I vow I am never going to stay with a man who is mean or uncaring. Why bother? What's the point? Mommy doesn't say anything to us about the marriage, even though she talks about everything else with us. I just don't get it. I don't have much to say to Daddy these days. What is there to say?

I live my life.

DAY BY DAY
I live
I eat
I dream
I survive

I've been writing a bunch of poems lately. Some of them are kind of morbid, but I also think they are really good. Mommy likes them, too. She encourages me to write some happy ones, also. I write when I feel something really intensely, I tell her.

JUDGMENT DAY

The line was long.

It went

Down the street

And around the corner

And down the block

And past all the houses and stores

And through states

Then countries

And across waters

To almost the end of the world.

And everyone waited

Some eagerly

Some patiently

Some reluctantly

But all, waiting.

But what they didn't know,

Was that when they reached the front of the line,

There wasn't anything there

And all their waiting

Had been

For

Nothing.

September 19, 1979 • I've decided Boston University is the college I want to attend. I am spending much time on my application. I can't wait. I think it is going to be great. I am not sure what I want to major in yet. There are so many things that interest me: English, psychology, sociology, law. It's tough to pick. I am not sweating it, though. I know there is time. Even if I go in as an undeclared major. There are several requirements all freshmen take. I can get those done, select a cross section of my interests, and then choose. Works for me. Some kids are really tripping about majors and stuff like that. But I know it will work out. I just want to go to BU; it feels like the perfect place for me.

Through my godmother, I got to speak about BU with Carol Jenkins, an anchorwoman for NBC News. She is a BU alumna. She was very encouraging and said that BU is especially strong in some of my areas of interest. Talking with her has only increased my desire to go there.

September 20, 1979 • Sitting on the train turns out to be a good place to write, when it doesn't jerk too much. I got an after-school job in the city, at B. Altman's on 34th Street. Three days a week, after school, so I am spending a lot of time on the train.

I work in Accounts Receivable. I'm having a great time, especially with the discount I get on almost everything in the store. I found out Daddy used to work at B. Altman's when he was young, after he'd just returned from the Korean War. I never knew that.

I still have my hair in braids. I love it this way. So does everyone else, now that they've gotten used to it.

September 22, 1979 • I can't believe it. After all these years, now that I finally got over my feelings for Nick (and replaced them with a crush on his friend Hugo), Nick likes me. He's not even being shy about it. He even told Crystal and Devon. In a way, I wish I could change my feelings and want to be with him. But after all those years of having a crush on him, I finally got over it. Life is strange and ironic. Of course, Hugo doesn't like me. At least he doesn't show it, even if we do laugh and joke a lot. This guy stuff is really confusing. Nick and I are still friends. We joke and talk. I just don't desire to go with him anymore.

The other day on the E train on the way to work, this guy was sitting right across from me, jerking off. I couldn't believe it. I had to wait till the next stop before I could change cars. You see everything on the train in the city. And I mean, everything.

September 23, 1979 • Sherry and I finally told Mommy how we feel about our family. We prefaced it by saying we don't get into grown-ups' business, but this truly affects us all. We told her how lousy things feel at home and how much we feel that Daddy just doesn't care about us. And how tired we are of the mean stuff he does and says and of feeling bad. We are practically to the point where either he goes, or maybe Sherry and I go.

"Why are you still together?" we ask her, even though it is hard to say. "Why don't you guys get a divorce? It seems like that makes more sense."

"I thought you girls were happy. I didn't want you not to have your father around or for us not to be a family," Mommy tries to explain. "He's never around anyway," we point out. "And when he is here, it doesn't feel good."

"Don't stay with him on our account," we say. We take care of each other, we three do. That's the way it's been for a long time anyway. Even if we still all live under the same roof most of the time.

October 4, 1979 • There's this new club on the Avenue that we have all been going to on the weekends. It's called Renaissance. We all go there to party together. Joyce comes too. She goes to Music and Art High School in the city and has continued to develop her art talent from our elementary school days. I'm glad we still hang out together.

We dance the freak and rock and stay till the place closes (at 2 A.M.). Mommy picks us up afterwards. The Renaissance is a pretty fly club. There are a lot of homeboys there trying to get a rap, some of whom are pretty rowdy. But there are also some guys there who are pretty cool. Plus, we always go with a bunch of our friends. Sometimes that doesn't daunt the homeboys. "Yo, Miss Lady" they say. What is that? Miss Lady. That sounds so dumb to me. If you don't answer, they change it to, "Yo, bitch."

I like all different kinds of music. Some of my friends think that is weird, but I don't care. My favorite radio station is 99X, even though it is WBLS that plays all the jams. I like 99X because I love singing songs like "Sailing," "Brandy" and even Barry Manilow's love songs. I like jams, too. I don't think there's anything wrong with liking lots of different styles. All-in-one me.

I've learned, though, over the years, that being your own person may have its own cost. But how I choose to react to people who view me differently, that is the power of my choice and what I want to pay or give. I am learning that I can deal with not only being myself, but however people choose to react. I can cope. It seems as though it is always something different anyway that folks are talking about and dealing with, whether it's cigarettes, or music, or dress, and what's down today is corny tomorrow.

In our school, it seems as if there are ways that black people dress and ways that white people dress. I like wearing different kinds of clothes. If you are black and you wear an outfit somebody thinks "isn't cool," they say you dress like you're a white girl. Or speak like one, for that matter. I find the whole concept of this separation ridiculous.

Sherry and I dress in whatever we feel like, and we don't care when somebody says, "Ya'll have on white-girl jeans." My own style feels good to me, and that's what is important.

Or when folks say that we aren't down, because we don't find the style attractive when the black guys wear Lee jeans hanging so low that we can see their multicolored nylon boxers. And then there's the white kids who get mad when a white kid hangs out with black kids.

The whole attitude is silly to me. I am looking forward to college, where I hope I don't have to deal with nonsense like this.

Meanwhile, I hold true to the song: I gotta be me. I'm glad I am comfortable in this space.

I see the world through my own eyes. After all, they are the only eyes I've got. Sometimes I am so busy focusing on the beauty of the world, Mommy says she worries I'll miss something, things I might need to know. She says again, that's why she sent me to public school and Sherry to private, because I needed a less sheltered environment to open my eyes. She says sometimes I need to speak up more, even with my friends. Like with Justine, who occasionally says things that are rather cruel, like teasing me about my choice in clothes. "If you don't stick up more for yourself, Justine will squish you like a marshmallow," Mommy says.

November 9, 1979 • Today I have realized that my whole life is changing. Now that Sherry has a boyfriend, things will be totally different. She's out of our CIA club. How will I be able to share with her my fears about never having a boyfriend? That no guy will ever really like me.

I like her boyfriend, Ben. She met him in the premed program. But I am worried that we won't be able to relate anymore. This is the biggest difference there has ever been between us, and it is a big difference. I still can't even imagine what it feels like to have a boyfriend. I feel so embarrassed by this and so tacky. I don't envy or feel jealous of Sherry; it's just that I wish we could share the experience. But we can't, and I am excluded. I guess it must be kind of like when one sister gets married. I know this sounds pessimistic, but I could always feel I was different. I think Sherry realizes how things are changing, and she is trying not to admit that to herself, and that's why she is still trying to be CIA, because she feels she is drifting away.

Who am I kidding trying to be a normal person? I feel as though I am one of those people on earth for a short time. When I feel this, I wonder if I am dramatizing from reading too many books or if it's really true. Sometimes I feel that I am in danger of becoming a totally imaginative person. I hope this is just a bad case of adolescence, I really do.

I hope that when I look back on this five years from now, I, too, can say how ridiculous, and let Sherry read this and maybe we'll laugh or cry and feel a little nostalgic (how corny). I hope that five years from now I don't read this and see how right I was.

I hope that life is not too cruel to me because I am either ridiculously sensitive or stupid.

I hope these thoughts I just had are only silly, childish, I won't even dignify them with the term "adolescent," fantasies.

December 13, 1979 • In chemistry I have made another new friend, Lincoln. He just moved here from California with his brother. He sits behind me in chem. Even though we both sit really close to the board, we can't see it too well. I don't like wearing my glasses, so I carry them with me. We pass my glasses back and forth to each other to read the board. It works pretty well. Lincoln is my lab partner. I like chemistry better than biology. In biology in tenth grade, I refused to dissect a frog. The teacher said if I didn't do it, I would receive an F for that day. So be it. It was worth the F.

Today was so funny. Usually, since Sherry's classes start about 45 minutes after mine, she walks up the hill with me and hangs out with our crew at Jamaica before walking over to Hillcrest High, about ten minutes away. This morning she came into chemistry for my first period class. We look so much alike, even more so these days, we decided to see if we could trick Mrs. Bradbury into thinking Sherry was me.

"Good morning, Mrs. B," Sherry said. "I'm here early for once!" "That's great, Sharon," Mrs. Bradbury says, "now take your seat." Sherry walks over to my seat amidst, "Hey, Sharon, good morning," said by some kids who have known me for years. Mission accomplished. Then laughing, Sherry leaves to go to school in time for her first period.

Oh, yeah, I got braces two months ago. I don't mind, though. I like them. They are closing my gap through which I used to be able to blow bubbles—gum bubbles and, in my grosser moments, spit bubbles. No more. Funny, I remember when Sherry and I used to want glasses and braces; now we've got both of them. I can't wait to get my contact lenses.

December 20, 1979 • In homeroom this year, I sit across from Nick and in front of this hardrock girl, Enid. Usually Enid and I get along OK, but for some reason today she is really mad at me. I think she kind of likes Nick, or maybe she guessed my homeroom buddy, Priscilla, and I were laughing about her.

"Look, bitch," Enid tells me, "you open your mouth, and I'll throw you out that window." I get ready to open my mouth really wide, like you do in the doctor's office, except I see Priscilla behind Enid wildly shaking her head, don't do it. I take her advice. But it is hard.

Enid acts so ignorant, Priscilla and I agree. Why'd it have to be all that? Priscilla thinks Enid likes Nick, and resents our friendship. Whatever, I think.

I've got hurts too, Enid, trust me. You aren't the only one.

DEAR GOD,
Sometimes, I talk to you
And ask you to make something really wonderful happen to me
And bring me something I'm really missing

And I tell myself I shouldn't ask you
Because what have I done for you?
I know you don't owe me anything
I guess if I were you, I wouldn't answer me either
Because, who am I?
Nobody.

January 11, 1980 • Crystal, Justine and I always write notes to each other. We've been doing this for years. Today I meet them in the hallway after homeroom.

Hang out with me and be late for fourth period, I ask them. We take our time walking down the hall.

My parents are getting a divorce, I blithely tell them. "Oh," they say. "You OK?" they ask. Yeah, I'm fine. Sherry and I are glad. At least it makes sense.

They nod. "We know what you mean," Justine says. We continue down the hall. Crystal holds my hand extra tight when she passes me her note as she goes into Spanish. I squeeze back, tight.

And run to humanities, my favorite class.

February 1, 1980 • My humanities teacher, Mrs. Nasence, is also my guidance counselor. She's kind of a soft-spoken white lady who typically lets Mr. Masters take the lead in humanities and do most of the theatrics. I think she was a literature major in college.

I tell her that BU is definitely where I plan to go, and I am waiting for my letter of acceptance from them. "I think you are better suited to go to a junior or city college," she tells me.

I am taken aback by her "counseling." I speak up for myself.

You have all of my grades and test scores, Mrs. Nasence. I always get 90s in your class, and I did really well on the SAT. I've been offered a full four-year engineering scholarship to Florida

A&M, and I don't even like math. I have a personal interview with Harvard. Why shouldn't I attend BU?

"No, you'll handle a junior college much better," she tells me. Whatever, I think. I'm going to BU, lady. I never feel the same about Mrs. Nasence again.

I tell Crystal and we laugh. Does Mrs. Nasence really think I am going to fall for that old one?

February 2, 1980 • Today we sent Pepper away. Rochdale finally said he's got to go. I wanted us to move, but Mommy said we can't afford it, and where would we go? I feel so awful; I love him and miss him so much. His new family says we can come visit him anytime and that he is still our dog, but it will never be the same. I just feel all around terrible.

Before, there were five of us in our family here; now there are only three.

Although I am now a finalist for a scholarship, it seems to me like what difference does that really make in my life? When I write down my most secret thoughts, even though I have fun at school, I still feel bad inside.

ALWAYS

Always is a beautiful word
It is forever
Infinite
A long time, longer than any of us can envision
Always is to me perfection
If one thing in my life can be
Always
Then I will be eternally happy.

February 22, 1980 • Time to buy prom tickets. I've not been invited by anyone to go. Still time is ticking by, life is going on even with all the weird stuff that happens. I am living my life. And doing my best to appreciate the laughter of the moment; when I'm laughing and it hurts, and when I'm laughing and it feels good.

March 3, 1980 • Our debutante cotillion is coming up. It's an African cotillion. Every week we have rehearsal. We march, parade, curtsey, and hustle to drum beats and Miriam Makeba. Then we each recite a piece we personally selected. My piece is by Langston Hughes:

I TOO SING AMERICA
I am the darker sister [I changed that from "brother"].
They send me to eat in the kitchen
When company comes,
But I laugh,
And eat well,
And grow strong
Tomorrow,
I'll be at the table when company comes
Nobody will dare say to me,
"Eat in the kitchen,"
Then.
Besides, they'll see how beautiful I am
And be ashamed—
I too am America.

March 29, 1980 • I called Nick. I also called Hugo. (Well actually, I was too shy to call Hugo, so Mommy called Hugo for me and pretended to be me. They had this quick silly conversation.)

Nick invited me roller-skating. We went to Skatetown USA. I went skating with Nick and Hugo (who was there, too). This girl Debra from school (who likes Nick) got there later; she was tacky. Later, on the train, Nick kissed me. I mean really kissed me. As in tongue kissed me. Quote of Debra: "Who you messing with, anyway, Nick or Hugo?" Yeah!

April 20, 1980 • I am thrilled. I am going to Boston University. I will be in the College of Liberal Arts. Crystal has decided to go to Hunter College in the city and stay with her dad. Nick is going to go to the University of Chicago, and Hugo will attend the University of Maryland. Justine has another year to go. I know this school won't be the same without us. But she's got Lincoln and some other close friends and a bunch of guys trailing behind her, so I know she'll be OK.

Crystal's boyfriend, Dazzlin Devon, has dropped out of school. He still goes with Crys and comes up to school to hang out. But he's given up on it. He's thinking about going into the Air Force. My old friends Tracy and Corey, from P.S. 131 days are planning on getting married this summer.

April 29, 1980 • We are all trying to get in as many great times as possible. Going to the Y all the time and dancing, shopping in the city and having bbq's at Crystal and Winston's house even though it's still a little cold outside. We blast our theme song "Ain't No Stoppin Us Now" and make up dances. In my quieter moments, it feels somewhat bittersweet, but I soak it all up and cherish it. These times we share.

Daddy now lives in the city. He is staying at his friend Archie's house. We talk to him once in a while or meet him for a movie. We don't talk much about what happened. It's kind of uncomfortable. I don't understand my father.

I told Daddy I am going to Boston University. He said, "Why do you have to go there?"

I said, because it's where I want to go. And if you don't get it, oh well.

At home, Rochdale has given us an eviction notice. Turns out Daddy wasn't paying the rent before he left, and if we don't pay the back months, they are going to evict us. Mommy is trying hard to scrape up the money, hocking jewelry, trying unsuccessfully to sell old fur coats and her treasured stamp collection from when she was a child. She even called Uncle James for help. He has a lot of money. But she doesn't know if he will decide to help or not. The plan is, if we get evicted, she will have to go and stay with her aunt in New Jersey, I will stay at Justine's apartment and Sherry will stay with Faith.

I am not a person
I am just a body with a face
I cannot feel anything
Because I have felt too much.

May 1, 1980 • Last night I started thinking about everything that's happened. I actually started crying. I realized that I hadn't cried about Daddy in all the time this happened. Not even when he said go to hell.

Then I did the thing that most helps me in life when I feel something so profoundly that I don't know how to contain my emotions. I wrote this poem. I don't know if I will ever show Daddy. But this one is for me.

DADDY'S GIRL
Daddies love their little girls
They always say that's true

But something tells me, that's not the case
Between me and you

And now you're saying
Oh that's cruel of course you've got my love
To which my only reply will be
The statement that's above

You showed every day the way you really feel
In a thousand and one ways, you proved my theories real
When I was young and I tried to hold you near
You left me for your own life, each year after year.

This life did not include me or my sister or my mother
To you we were invisible your love all given to others
It wasn't that you hit us or drove us to despair
The simple fact of life is that you were never there

And now that I am sixteen, and looking back on life
It hurts to say that you were not a husband to your wife
Or a father to us, that is what we desired
We sometimes used to wish that you would be fired

I used to hope and pray
That someday you would change
That we could all be together is what I would arrange
I used to wish that I could have a loving father
To whom I would not seem such an eternal bother

I never felt you cared or really wanted me
To you I was just another kid in the world, you see

A little less important and a little more annoying
Though the last thing any of us was is cloying

I never used to realize how deeply I felt
How terrible the cards in life I'd been dealt
Only recently have I realized how painful the injury
My life with you has been to me.

I needed a father how much I never knew
But then, why weren't you there
What did I do?

I know I'm not the best person in the world
I'm not an angel or a boy, I'm just a girl
Who needed a father and still needs one now
But I know it's too late for that anyhow

So that's one thing in life, I know I have missed
I never had a daddy who hugged and kissed

The many things you have done
That shall forever go unnamed
Have hurt me deep inside
So that I feel I am lamed

But please don't ever try to make it all up
I could not bear to taste such a long overdue cup
Maybe you feel that you have been wronged
But if that's the case, why not the talk for which I've longed?

I think it's so unfair
How you have been to all of us

Why couldn't you be a little loving or a little just
You didn't show an interest
You didn't share with me
I think you thought of us as pests
And living with us a penalty

I think that now you're gone
You won't miss us at all
For what were we to you
Except pains you'd sometimes call

A little exaggerated, you might say
Well that's how I feel
Right now, today.

It used to hurt an awful lot
Though I never thought about it
And now it hurts even more
And the pieces still don't fit

You've been like this always
I just want to know why
I just want the truth
Not an excuse or a lie
Is it all our fault
I'll say it again

What did we do?
Was it us, or is it you?

And now that I am almost
But not quite grown

I think of the things that I have always known
Daddies love their little girls
They always say that's true
But something tells me
That's not the case
Between me and you.

May 2, 1980 • We did it! Or should I say Mommy did it. We can stay and keep the apartment. Mommy managed to gather enough money to satisfy Rochdale. Thank God.

I created a new motto to take the place of CIA: You only become a Somebody when you realize that you already are.

May 15, 1980 • Nick called me and invited me to the prom. Only one day before prom night. I was unsure what to do, but Mommy and Sherry were standing beside me, nodding their heads vigorously. Go, go.

So I said yes.

Mommy and I raced out shopping the following afternoon.

May 16, 1980 • I wore a beautiful white dress, really sexy, with crimson flowers in my hair, and he wore a white tuxedo. He looked so handsome. We took pictures before at my house, in the living room. Even Sherry thought Nick looked really good. She still thinks he's kind of doofey, after all these years. (Smile.)

All of us were there at the prom together, even Justine, who of course had a date with one of the seniors. Afterward, we went out and partied all night at a club in the city. Nick and I did a lot of kissing. It felt really good. I am getting to be pretty good at this!

Graduation is right around the corner, and I can't believe how fast time is flying by.

May 17, 1980 • It was afternoon before I woke up. Sherry, Mommy, and I sat around the kitchen table, drinking tea, as I told them the story. Just as we've always done. Sherry has a date later with her new boyfriend, Keith. I am going to chill out and just relax. Nick invited me to the movies tonight. Mommy is studying for her test on Monday. School is going great for her and she has picked up more classes.

On the radio, station 99X, the Beatles' "The Long and Winding Road" played softly in the background.

Pack...

IT'S TOUGH TO DESCRIBE WHAT I LEARNED TO pack. What I want to say is: Pack "rolling with the punches." Working to be adaptable and flexible wherever I am in life. I learned in those years so much about not being attached to one way of living, or doing, or getting things done. To handle change. Damn, that's it . . .

Pack Change

It may sound strange, but it's coming no matter what. It always does. So I learned to pack the ability to be *with* change, instead of fighting against it. I've learned to embrace change when it occurs, and not to resist it. It makes the journey so much smoother, full of discovery and perhaps even more peaceful. Change is a natural part of life. I have learned to cherish yesterday, while understanding and accepting that tomorrow may be very different. Change comes to us all, how we greet it . . . therein lies our choice.

4

Uncharted Territory

September 2, 1980 • Halfway to Boston the bus broke down. Greyhound buses aren't supposed to do this, I thought. How many minutes or hours we were stopped, I had no idea. It was more pleasant to dream, think, and sleep than to watch the bus driver pace back and forth in the dried weeds on the side of the highway. Gradually I became aware that someone was staring at me. I opened my eyes.

"Hello," my seatmate said. "I couldn't help but notice you were smiling in your sleep."

I felt embarrassed, but I answered.

I guess I was thinking about school. I'm on my way to Boston University. I'm a freshman. I probably sat up a little straighter when I said that part.

"How exciting. Quite a way to begin," she observed, looking outside at the bus driver stubbing out his latest cigarette.

Yes, I guess so, I replied laughing. Not exactly the way I imagined it.

"Life seldom is," she answered. "I'm Thelma."

Sharon, I offered and took a good look at her for the first time. It felt funny to be calling a lady who looked a little younger than my mom by her first name. I called my mother's friends Mrs. Watson, Mrs. Lockhardt, and Mrs. Steiner. I really am growing up.

"So I guess you are very excited about college?" Thelma asked.

Yes, I am. I couldn't think of anything to add to that. There were all these thoughts bouncing around inside of me, but how could I explain them to this lady?

"You know, Sharon, my college years were the four best years of my life." Thelma shifted heavily in her seat, but when she smiled, I could almost see the long-ago kid in her looking back at me.

Why? I asked her. Something in the way she said it made me want to . . . what's that expression we learned last year? Seize the day!

"College was a time full of"—she paused, her pink-colored lips stuck together as she searched for the word—"discovery. Sharon, keep your eyes open in school. Not just so that you can see what's in front of you, but so that you can really be open to exploring all that life has to offer."

Too deep for me, I thought. That's what Justine would laughingly say, right about now. Me, I kept listening.

"What are you majoring in?"

Man. Here we go with that question again. I told her the truth.

I haven't declared my major yet. I have all these different things I dream about doing. I haven't decided which to choose. I've envisioned myself a sociologist, a dancer, a model, a lawyer and a doctor. Actually, several interests inspire me, so I set up my classes to get a taste of each. I guess the main thing that is calling to me is working to help people.

"Don't let anybody tell you that it's not OK to take your time making up your mind," she said. "I know you didn't ask for my advice, but allow me to share it."

I smiled when she said that. It seemed to me that's what she had been doing all along.

"Remember, sometimes advice comes from the strangest places. It's good that you are open-minded toward your future. Take your time and make up your own mind. College is a time to learn your-self and, in learning yourself, to figure out where you are headed. And to have fun with it."

Thank you, Thelma, I said. For some reason, her words made me want to cry. They made me feel good and scared and excited all at the same time.

The conversation was so absorbing, I hadn't realized we were moving once again.

Hey, it's Boston. We're finally here.

September 5, 1980 • I keep thinking about Thelma's words. They have given me plenty to reflect on. Here's this life thing, with so many (to be corny about it) ups and downs and twists and turns. If life is a journey, what does that really mean?

So, OK, let's say we are each . . . on a journey. Sometimes it seems as if the moment encompasses all. Or is it that a series of moments combine to create a life? How much does each instant define the sum total of one's existence? What are the points in time that really don't matter, and where are the junctures that can change your life forever? And is there really any such thing?

When all is said and done and it's your last day on earth, do you really ever know where the importance in each action lay and how it all fits together? I think what I get from my conversation with Thelma is that, maybe, what is important is to appreciate each moment from the beginning, for what it is in its given time, and to value all time equally, giving it all you've got.

September 10, 1980 • The hall of the dormitory was full of stu-dents rushing to and from dinner. Warren Towers dormitory, or the zoo as it is more commonly known, is a sprawling building with three towers, each of which soars 18 stories high, with count-less dorm rooms on each floor. I live in B tower.

Heading back to my room after a mediocre turkey dinner, I suddenly thought I recognized someone.

During the summer I'd met Sarah, a girl from New Jersey whom I first noticed across a crowded room. She was easy to spot because we'd been the only two blacks there. I recalled her also because although we'd talked for only a few minutes, I'd liked her tremendously. She had this special way about her. Just being in her presence, it was almost like you couldn't help but feel good.

It was Sarah. I was pretty sure. I raced after her and caught up just as she was about to enter the C tower elevator.

Do you remember me? We met this summer. I'm Sharon, I said. You're name's—

"Sarah," she said and smiled.

It's good to see you again, Sarah, I answered. And we began to talk. After a few minutes, I asked her the good old question: What's your major?

"I'm undeclared," she said. She sounded comfortable with that, too. Not tripping over it as some kids did.

So am I, I told her.

Kindred spirits.

October 8, 1980 • I can't believe I've been here more than a month now. It seems like just yesterday that Mommy, Daddy and Sherry drove up to help me get settled and bring me my things. I'm glad that even though Mommy and Daddy are divorced, they still work together around family things like graduation and coming up to see me start college. Daddy has his own place in the city. In a way, it feels better than when Daddy lived with us. But I don't know how it feels to be back home, as Sherry is now, with the family at home being down to two people. That's got to feel different. Of course, this does, too. But here, everything is new.

Right now, I'm sitting at the desk in my cinder-block dorm room. It's a far cry from Sherry's and my beautiful green and canary-yellow room, back home, but I like it. I don't have biology for another forty-five minutes, so I can keep writing.

This campus is incredibly large. It stretches from one end to the other of the main thoroughfare, Commonwealth Avenue. My biology class is in the College for Liberal Arts, although everybody just calls it CLA, right across the street from my dorm. My anthropology class, which meets directly after, is all the way down at the other end of campus, so I have to go tearing out of biology to make it in time for anthropology. I should have scheduled that better. Oh well, I didn't know. Next time I will.

I really like this whole college setup. Here they give you a syllabus, you buy your textbooks (which are really expensive, I don't like that part), and they tell you what is required of you at the beginning of the semester. Then you take it upon yourself to do it or not.

Much more responsibility as well as independence. I like it. The class discussions are pretty stimulating as well. It just seems as if there is a lot more freedom and flexibility here as to how one can live life. And getting a chance to figure out more of who I am and what I prefer, not just classes, but my way of being, is a great feeling. Self-determination.

Oh. Got to go. I haven't looked at the clock for a while. Class starts in two minutes. Man, I'm going to be late again. Some habits are hard to break.

One thing I am definitely getting better at, though, is talking with guys!

TODAY

I walked out on yesterday.
I packed my memories into a big box
And placed them in the farthest corner of the attic

And then I opened the door
And let in
Tomorrow

October 16, 1980 • For the first time in my life, I really felt a guy's crush on me. This guy was crazy about me. Jason Baker. Thing is, I liked him, but I wasn't crazy about him. But I enjoyed his company.

Unfortunately, one day he came by when I was in a really silly mood. Not too unusual. I was eating Oreo cookies, which was unusual.

I offered him one, saying an Oreo for an oreo? I was only kidding, calling him an oreo totally in jest.

He left without response.

How was I to know that I had hit one of the sorest spots in his life? Turns out his dad is black and his mom, white.

So in his life, this word oreo had taken on painfully special meaning. (Although me, with my logical self, argued that the term oreo means white on the inside, black on the outside.)

Really, though, thing was, it had been the source of much pain for Jason growing up, and I guess there were lots of kids who had misused the word. It should stay a word that refers only to an edible cookie. I knew all about pain growing up and about being teased. And called names, even oreo, by kids who considered my speech, or dress, or way of relating, different.

Jason didn't tell me what had happened himself. I walked around in blissful ignorance, unaware of what had happened. The way I found out was from one of the busy-bodies on campus. It seems I had a whole crew of people angry with me for insulting and hurting Jason.

When I found out, I was in tremendous pain. I tried to explain to him and eventually to some of that crew that it was nothing more than a horribly stupid joke, that I didn't even know about his background, that I had no wish to hurt him and how sorry I was, that I knew what it felt like to be cruelly teased, and that that wasn't who I was, either. Not somebody who wanted to intentionally hurt people, and not an oreo.

Jason accepted my apology, although I don't think he will ever feel the same about me again.

October 18, 1980 • Tonight, a big tough girl who has a black belt in tae kwon do and a crush on Jason knocked on my dorm door. Letting her in probably wasn't the smartest move. But there she stood, center stage in my room, as I sat perched on my bed.

"When I heard what you said to Jason, I wanted to kick your ass," she informed me. Pounding her fist into her palm for emphasis.

It wasn't clear to me that she had decided she wasn't going to pursue that course of action.

I reiterated what I had told everyone else. By now I was growing offended and hurt that no one, with the possible exception of Jason, seemed to want to take my word for it. Apparently it was easier to believe I was a bitch.

After outstaying her welcome, she left.

I have to find a place inside myself to deal with all this and to accept the fact that I hurt someone severely.

And to accept that hurting someone that I care about, even when I didn't intend it, is a part of life. And finally, to understand that even though compassion might be in my heart, it doesn't mean that I will receive it from others.

MISCONCEPTION

TO WHOM IT MAY CONCERN

Dedicated to all those who thought life would treat them as they treated life. And to all those who have yet to find out, this isn't the truth.

I had a misconception that the world was a beautiful place
That everything in it was sincere, honest, and good
Reality made me realize my naiveté.
I'd go back
If I could.

October 19, 1980 • But there's only forward. Keep going. Sharon, keep going. Greet life as it comes. Here you are at college, the bastion of knowledge. And you're learning. Understanding yourself and some of the finer points of comprehending that, in life, in a moment you can hurt someone and then have to be with that. Facing up to the truth of yourself and your actions and then being true to that as well. Appreciating who you are and what the world is around you and how you contribute to that, for better or for worse.

November 1, 1980 • Some weekends we walk along the Charles River, watching the students in crew. I remember loving to row at Girl Scout camp in our little rowboats, nothing like the vigorous rowing I observe these students doing.

We walk on down the river, stopping, playing, and laughing during study breaks. This time of year in Boston, it has already become quite cold. We can see our breath rising in the air as we run.

"We" is the circle of friends I have made here. Sarah, Tamara from Seattle—another girl who loves to write poetry with whom I have become close friends—Will Joe from Texas, Phillip from the Bronx, and Alicia from Atlanta, to name only some of our crew.

Sarah, Tamara, and I have also become friends with a really quiet, nice, sweet guy who doesn't hang out with the crew much. His name is Henry, but he told us his parents call him Smooge. What kind of dumb nickname is that? we wonder. But we all like to be with him anyway.

November 2, 1980 • Saturday night we hung out in Sarah's dorm lounge on 16. I had bad cramps and lay on the floor curled up. Henry petted my face comfortingly as we listened to music from my favorite movie, *Fame,* and just chilled. I love days like this. Minus the cramps, it is perfect.

I spend a lot of time dancing, just listening to music and dancing to songs like my newest theme song, Irene Cara's "Out Here On My Own," from *Fame.* Kind of modern free-form dancing, the way I always have at home.

Dancing is almost like poetry to me. I can feel the music so inherently that dancing can finely tune my emotions. I'm happy that here at BU, I continue to have the space in my life to dance. I even dance in front of Henry, I feel just that comfortable with him and with myself.

Still our crew has been spending lots of time dancing, as in "jamming." It's funny when I think about how far I've come from the "make you or break you" party Mommy and Daddy made me go to.

We always get "dressed" when we go out. Sexy dresses, tight pants, and gorgeous suits. We travel to parties all over Boston: Harvard, Tufts, Boston College, and MIT; pretty much every weekend there are tons of parties. We try not to miss any of the really hot ones. So far, we are doing a pretty good job.

At most of these parties there is plenty of alcohol. I don't drink. I've never really tried alcohol. I remember when I went to Justine's sweet sixteen party back at Jamaica and there was a champagne toast, I snuck and poured my champagne out.

My buddy from Texas, Will Joe, drinks a lot. He really knows how to put it away. He said he was going to take Sarah and me out drinking. Really school us. "OK, we're game," we said; we thought it would be fun.

November 5, 1980 • Last night, Will Joe took us to a Chinese restaurant where they have huge drinks called scorpion bowls. We sat in a booth at the restaurant, amidst burgundy walls and lots of mirrors. Each with a long straw. Sip and sip and sip.

"This tastes pretty good," I said. "You can barely taste the alcohol," Sarah agreed.

After a while, I was definitely starting to feel it. We did a lot of laughing. This is fun, I thought. Will Joe kept teasing Sarah and me. He said we were drunk even though we had only had a few sips each. "No, we're nottttttt," we said ending on a screech, as we laughed and tripped our way to the bathroom. I did feel kind of funny.

We headed back to the table. It was empty. The bowl that is. Will Joe wanted to order another one.

No way," Sarah and I said. One was enough.

The three of us lurched out of the restaurant. Sarah and I almost fell onto a parked car. Will Joe was so strong, he pulled us off the car with one hand on each of us, and stood us steady on our feet.

"Taxi," we all called. It would have been a long, unsteady walk back to Warren Towers. On the ride back, Will Joe threw up out the window of the taxi.

November 10, 1980 • Sometimes I get homesick. I miss Mommy and Sherry. Even though I have made some wonderful friends here, I miss those all-day pajama Sundays with Sherry and Mommy. We talk on the telephone a lot. I try to tell them all about life here at BU. Some of it, like studying biology and knowing I don't want to be a doctor (someone else may have the blood, guts and glory) I can explain easily. Other things are much harder to convey, like since I am "out here on my own," what does that really mean?

When I am feeling lonely, I am so thankful for my poetry and for this book to write in. I keep it in a safe place here in my room, my own personal treasure. This book and Raggedy Andy. He is now much the worse for wear. Mommy had to sew him a new shirt since the old one got so tattered and worn. All that love, you know.

THE LIGHT
In our house
The light is always on
It's there waiting for us
When we come home
And when we are away
The light is always on
So that we can find our house
Among all the others in
This mysterious world.

November 11, 1980 • I still have never had a boyfriend, even though I am seventeen years old and a freshman in college. I now am really comfortable being close friends with guys. But I still am nervous trying to talk with a guy I really like. I've been on a few dates and kissed and even made out a little, but what I want is someone to whom I am really special, and him to me. I feel funny about never having had that. To tell the truth, I feel embarrassed. I don't feel as tacky as I used to, and I have definitely resigned from the CIA, and I realize some guys find me attractive. But when am I going to meet the guy who truly likes me, and I him . . . at the same time? I finally told Sarah the truth, that I have never had a boyfriend before, but I haven't told anybody else. I pour out my dreams into my poetry. I wrote this poem that I have shared with no one.

US
Yesterday we hadn't met
We were two separate beings moving on our own individual course

Today, I'll never forget
We collided, and our paths turned as one toward a common place.
Tomorrow has not come yet
But when it does we will be there to greet it
Together

November 14, 1980 • I did it! I published a poem.

I joined *Blackfolk*, which is just what it sounds like, the black student newspaper. All my passionate imaginings of love have gone into my poetry. Into my poems, like "Loving You." I got up the courage to submit it, and they published it in this month's edition! People have been coming up to me and telling me how much they like it. One girl even hung it up on the mirror in her dorm. I am so excited. I've shared my poetry. Yeah.

LOVING YOU
If you leave me here tomorrow
I will follow you today
If you try to say good-bye
I will only try to stay
If you walk I'll be behind you
Or better yet
By your side
For we'll always be together
Be the distance short or wide
If you should ever leave me
Who knows then what I would do
But I know I'll live forever
Or as long as I have you.

March 12, 1981 • Hanging out in the ghetto. That's right. That's the nickname for the area of the Warren Towers cafeteria where many of the black folks eat. It was nicknamed "the ghetto" by black folks, as far as I can tell. I don't know how far back the name goes in Warren Towers' history, but that's what we call it.

I have developed a system for dinner. I call it my salad system. Salad has become my favorite meal. I make a huge salad from the salad bar, then I go over to the deli section and get a plate with turkey and cheese and add that to my salad. Voila! Chef's salad for dinner each night.

Tonight's conversation, as it often is, was about pledging. Dino, a junior who is a Sigma, was in the midst of discussing the merits of becoming a Sigma Dove.

"Being a Dove is a very unique opportunity," Dino was saying.

"Nah, man. Don't listen to him, my sisters. Why be a dove when you can be an angel?" was the smooth retort from Vincent, an Alpha who was espousing the merits of being an Alpha Angel.

Both the Doves and the Angels, as near as I can understand, are the girls' support groups for the fraternity guys. They help the guys out while they are on line, hide them out from the big brothers, get them meals, and so on. In turn, they are honored as Doves, Angels and so forth. Not for me, I am thinking. If I am going to go through all that trouble, I might as well pledge a sorority and be a full-fledged member in my own right. There are some girls who are Doves and Angels and Sweethearts (Kappa Sweethearts, that is) whom I really like and respect, but it is easy for me to conclude that I am going to have to pass on this one.

While the guys went on rapping, I talked with Onida, a senior who was the head of her sorority pledge line. She is an AKA. Her best friend, Deloris, was sitting beside her. Deloris is a junior who is currently the president of BU's Delta chapter. They're an unlikely combination, but they are best friends.

As the three of us sat twirling limp spaghetti (I gave in and tried the spaghetti in addition to my salad tonight), we talked about pledging.

Onida said, "My sorors are my girls. I know I can count on them no matter what."

Deloris added, "Pledging my sorority is an opportunity to accomplish some really positive goals with some very committed sisters."

When I was in high school, I was a member of the national sorority of Phi Delta Kappa, an educational sorority. I was in the high school chapter called the Xinos. In fact, I held an office. I liked the principles of the sorority, committed to education and excellence and helping the community. I didn't like the pomp and circumstance; the pledging, paddles and listening to big sisters. Even when I became a big sister, the rituals still didn't call to me.

I explained this to Onida and Deloris. To tell you the truth, I finished, I find the joking sorority membership in "Me Phi Me" suits me better. Most of my life I have felt like such an individualist. The idea of pledging, being on line, and adhering to the arbitrary rules of the big sisters just doesn't appeal.

"It's not like that," Onida and Deloris affectionately chided me. But for me, it is.

It just feels a bit confining, I said, and in an odd sort of way, exclusive.

The vibe of exclusivity, uniformity within each sorority, and separation from the others, that's the part I don't like.

Ultimately, I have decided that none of these groups are for me.

I like to be silly or make baby voices or act crazy and not follow conventions. I don't like to wear socks in the Boston winter, and I don't mind if my jeans aren't pressed or if folks criticize my becoming best friends with a guy like Will Joe, who isn't considered cool. Life is however we each choose to live it, I have come to believe.

And since my childhood was a place where I traveled a road that felt distinctly unconventional at times, and played and lived many a fantasy of my own creation, I see no reason to totally release these dreams in exchange for living in the real world 24–7 now. I'll keep traveling this journey with my vision of how I want it to be. A bit of imaginary worlds never hurt anybody.

ON SEEING LIFE

I stood while they kept walking
I ran while they stopped to rest
I smiled while they kept on talking
We who skip enjoy life the best
I smile when rain kisses my face
I turn cartwheels in grass wet or dry
They frown and quicken their pace
And condemn me as they pass me by
I don't ask you to try it my way
Please continue your life at a hum
But I choose to embrace life with a roar everyday
"We are marching to a different drum."

April 12, 1981 • Another blind date. After eleventh grade, maybe I should have left blind dates alone. Again, the guy was certainly fine. Again, I felt inept. Tamara hooked it up with her boyfriend, Charles, at Harvard, and this classmate, who is a friend of his, a sophomore named Greg.

We went out for scorpion bowls. I hadn't had one since the time Will Joe, Sarah, and I had our "adventure." Come to think of it, I haven't had any alcohol to drink before or since then.

Charles teased me a lot. Greg seemed really cool and nice, and older. I tried to take only a few sips of the scorpion, but I still felt weird as we walked back to Greg and Charles' dorm. Tamara went with Charles to his room, which left me with Greg in his. I recall trying to focus on talking to Greg as he showed me some pictures in an album.

I don't remember anything else until I woke up the next morning curled up asleep on top of his bed, still in my skirt, sweater, tights, and shoes. I was alone in the room. I found out later that Greg slept in the dorm lounge and made his two roommates do the same.

I feel so mortified. And so young.

May 5, 1981

Dear Sherry,

Great news. I am transferring into the School of Public Communications ("SPC"). I've decided to become a broadcast journalism major. Remember my friend Tamara, who writes poetry (and who hooked me up on that wack date)? She is in SPC. I spent a lot of time talking with people in that program about their classes and career aspirations.

I've come to realize that this is what I want to do. I am a natural for a major in communications, I believe. I love communications, to speak and converse with others and the exchange of information. I have a huge curiosity about the world and the people that inhabit it; and I've loved to write all my life. Also, I believe that through a career in journalism, I'll be able to help people and to make a positive difference. I have a lot to learn about this curriculum, but this is a step in the right direction. OK, I know this is starting to sound like one of my essays, but I am so excited about all the possibilities that exist in this giant step I am taking.

The requirements for transferring to SPC were more competitive than if I'd applied there originally, straight out of high school. That was kind of scary. But I've been admitted!

Anyway, sending you a big hug and kiss.

Your sister,

Sharon

June 23, 1981 • Hey Justine, I can't wait to see you. It's great to be home, I shouted, leaving a message on Justine's answering machine. More and more people are starting to get them. I haven't talked with Crystal in quite a while. It seems as though we've been growing apart since graduation. I miss her, but I guess I've come to understand that we are all constantly growing, sometimes in different directions.

Tonight, though, I am going to the movies with Nick. He is home from college, too. I got a job doing car insurance research part-time. The rest of the time, I plan on having a blast this summer.

Nick and I were really happy to see each other. He looks good. More mature. I guess I do, too.

"Wow," Nick said, "you put on a little weight."

The freshman ten pounds, I answered.

"I like it." He checked me out approvingly in my tight pink pants. "Before, you were sooooooo skinny."

What am I now? I asked.

"Thin," Nick smiled.

After the movie, we came back to my house to hang out in the living room. We talked about the past.

"I always liked you," Nick told me, looking me directly in the eye. "You were always hiding behind Crystal and then Justine."

I was so surprised I didn't know what to say. Nick has a girlfriend in college now, and I am happy for him. Our time has certainly passed. The crush feelings of my growing-up years are gone. I like him very much as a friend. I am glad to know after all this time that he really and truly liked me, too.

After Nick left, I sat looking in the mirror. I saw my face as I am now. Intense big dark eyes staring back at me. The same eyes of little Sharon and junior high school Sharon, who dreamt about Nick for so long. Did you hear that, Sharon? I asked my reflection. Junior high Sharon stared back at me, eyes open in wonderment. Nick likes me? She asked softly. I smiled and gave her a kiss on the cheek. Tonight was for you, kid, I told her. Then lovingly tucking her in to rest, I hit the sack.

July 25, 1981 • Yeah! Turning eighteen. I can't believe it! I am still in shock from my surprise party! They really tricked me. Justine invited me over to her house to spend the night and visit and to go to a picnic the next day. Even though the next day was my birthday, I figured OK, I don't have any big plans. When we got out to the park, looking for Justine's friends. I heard this huge shout.

"Surprise!"

Everybody was there. I'll never forget it as long as I live. My buddies from high school: Nick, Hugo, Joyce, Toni . . . my buddies from college James and Philip, everybody. I feel so incredibly loved.

All my dear family and friends. Mommy and Sherry told me all the great stories afterward, of how long they had planned, and all the finagling they had done to pull it off. They really outdid themselves. Daddy was there and in on it, too. Even some of the dear families from ballpark days. It felt like one of those once in a lifetime moments. Like "this is your life, Sharon Simpson."

Now I am eighteen. Never to be a child again. I am an adult. I wonder what that means, and what the future holds.

Pack Zest

A ZEST FOR LIFE.

A hunger and excitement and enthusiasm for living. A sense of discovery. Of being open to all that life has to offer and giving it my best. When I feel that I have succeeded and when I feel that I have failed. Pack Zest. That thrill of life as exploration . . . sticking my tongue out to taste it. And with this exhilaration, the recognition of myself as sojourner, on my life's journey.

First, I learned to pack Heart: empathy, courage and spirit. Next was Originality, the ability to be my own unique self. Third, the packing of Change, flexibility and rolling with the punches; being able to deal with Change and embrace it, rather than fight against it.

What's next then? How I take it all on . . . with Zest! Use the zest of an orange or lemon in cooking, and it adds flavor. Packing Zest adds an exuberant twist to the journey.

5

Dreams Amidst Moments of Reality

October 29, 1981 • I don't know how I can even write this. How should I phrase it? Well, here goes. I did it. I don't know. I am so confused. I have no idea how I feel. What was it? Where am I now? I lost it in college. Wow. I'm glad it was in our beautiful room.

I guess I should talk about it just so I can always remember it exactly. I just went back and read all the other entries in this journal over the years. Boy, have I changed. It was really interesting to read. It's funny how now I can answer so many of my past questions, and I have so many more.

Here I am in my sophomore year at college. It's a Thursday night around midnight, and I am sitting in the B tower study lounge writing this because I need the anonymity (or however you spell it) of being alone.

Can't I ever let myself be happy and not think? No matter what, I always put myself into a storybook.

Right now I feel dizzy; it's that feeling I get when I just know something could not really have happened, and it did. I can't place the time I had that feeling last. Oh well, what does it matter?

Sometime might have been my first kiss, when Mario kissed me. Who the hell knows? That's all behind me now.

Well, now let me try to be honest with myself so that I can sort out my mind. It will be funny to look back on this ten years from now. I wish it were ten years later, in a way. Still, then I might wish I were here. I remember Christopher asking me to write him a poem. I guess I should, now! I wonder what it's reception will be.

Anyway, in short, tonight I lost my virginity. (Another gross word.) Sure, I know people do that every day, but this is me.

Am I trying to be blasé about this? That is what I'm being, but that doesn't seem like me. I think it's just my mind protecting me. It's funny, as Sarah says, I'm usually so sure about everything. I don't know, Christopher tells me "don't be such a pessimist," but I can't help it.

So let me introduce Christopher to you, my dear journal. I can always count on you to be there. His name is Christopher Quinlan; he's eighteen, too. I wish I could say I know him completely, but I don't. He remembers meeting me last year. His sister is in my class. Chris says I stayed on his mind all this time. I know we have a lot of potential and that I like him a lot, but it was just too early, mentally. I shouldn't have given in. Maybe I was just tired of being Miss Innocent. I don't know. Even though actually I still am. I can't say what it felt like because I'm not sure. That's a shame. I don't think I was in the right mood. Something tells me that's not all there is to it.

I'm not upset. I think I am just being dramatic about it. But that's because that's what it is supposed to be, and it wasn't. Today I'm going to buy a Harlequin and lose myself in it.

Maybe deep down I'm not the sensitive person I thought I was. God, I hope things work out for me.

I don't really know how it happened. In my bed in Tamara's

and my beautiful, rainbow-filled room (although the beauty of the room didn't really move me at the time).

Christopher says his mind is all clear now. (He's had his relief.) Me, my mind is all screwed up and shadowed. Which just goes to show I don't trust him; he's right.

After it happened and he left, I put on "Oh, No" by the Commodores (will I remember that song?). And I held Raggedy Andy and cried. Then I thought, nobody will come to me right now. But there was a knock on the door, and Christopher came back, because he forgot his belt. But I think really just to see me. He hugged me again and left for his dorm. Maybe that was the best thing about the night.

I called Sarah. She was the first person I told. God, I wish my Sherry were here to talk. I know I will tell Mommy, too. Because I love her and I want us to keep being close, I've got to share this.

Still, I want the flowers and the cards and the walks. He doesn't take me out yet.

My problem is, I am in love with the whole idea of romance. Whether I play the part of heroine and it's tragic or wonderful doesn't matter to me as long as I am in the book. Which is how I ruin myself. Still it could have been much worse or much better.

I know it's my fault. I just wish there was somebody to hug me and hold me who didn't care what I did and just loved me because I'm me. Did I waste what was mine to give? Was it appreciated? By me or by him?

GROWING UP

When I was young and very small
I always used to wonder
How it felt to be an adult and over age, not under
To make decisions and rule my life
To be the cause of my own joy or strife

To have responsibility
To know people saw an adult in me

I used to think that I'd know then
What the world was all about
That when I reached that magic age
All questions would work out

And now that I am older
I look at myself in wonder
To see that now I wish sometimes
I was not of age, but under.

November 1, 1981 • I spent a soothing day with Alicia. She is a junior whom I met at minority orientation at the beginning of the year. She transferred here from a small school in Maryland whose name I can't remember.

Anyway, I like spending time at her house. She has a real apartment and is beautiful and has her shit together.

"You have to add just the right amount of chili powder," Alicia instructed me as together we made her famous tacos and bean sauce. She was sharing her secret recipe with me. I love to cook. The only thing more fun than making these tacos was, yes, predictably, eating them.

Alicia talked to me about men and sex and life.

I told her that I only want to ever sleep with one man, the man I marry. But I am not sure whether I would want to marry Chris. I don't know him well enough.

She looked at me kind of strangely after I said that. I don't know what she was thinking. But she said, "Don't worry Sharon. It will work itself out."

February 12, 1982 • Hi. It's a long time since I've written. I'm very happy now. I love Christopher.

I've been meaning to write for a long time. Maybe when you're super happy, you lose the inspiration.

Chris and I spend so much time together these days. Our relationship has really developed, and I can talk to him about everything.

The thing is, when Chris and I go out to the movies or to dinner or wherever, I always feel his love. If I am making a funny baby voice or wearing my funky red socks with the black lace from the Village, he loves me and is proud of me. He accepts me for who I am, loves me for it. He loves my quirkiness and my serious side. He listens to my poetry, encourages me to sing. And while I was still coming to terms with our being in a relationship, the emotional side and the intimacy of it, he didn't give up on loving me. He was patient and stayed with me. He didn't measure what I was ready to give. And, now that I am more comfortable with "us," and with making love, I have great joy in our being together. And . . . it feels great.

Chris has a nickname for me; he calls me his Spunky.

We spent part of Christmas vacation together in New York. Mommy, Sherry and Daddy all like Chris.

Lately, we've been working on my video production assignments for broadcasting class. Even when it's dumb stuff like agreeing to star in one of the video stories I created, Chris is there. Since he's an engineering major, I can't help him much there. But I go to his track practices, and we have even been performing dances together (well, trying to) in the Black Drama Collective.

Life can be difficult, but it's great.

FOR CHRISTOPHER
ON LOVING

If love were especially created
For people like us just to find
Then I am not surprised at the moments
Love is constantly upon my mind.
Though our meeting occurred in the present
Perhaps it took place long before
Our lives were entwined by some favor of fate
Which strengthened our love all the more
As I look into your eyes which reflect
The love that you see in my own
I am sure that though sometimes we must be apart
We are each of us never alone
Love has added such dimension to living
Cleared my eyes where before I was blind
It has shown me to the true meaning of giving
And put you constantly upon my mind.

February 23, 1982 • This year Tamara and I have a room together on the SPC floor. Our room is a big double, reserved mostly for sophomores. As sophomores on a floor of mostly freshman, we get to share our experiences with the new students. In fact, we are SPC Peer Advisors, a task we are both really enjoying.

We've taken plenty of time to decorate our room and to make it mystical and joy-filled. We've been tacking our poems up on the bulletin board, mixed in with inspirational quotes, pictures, and other items. My favorite poem is Maya Angelou's "Still I Rise."

I think about Maya's words often, think about my life as a kid and this new strange adult thing. Still, I'll rise. Keep it in my brain. Keep it in my spirit.

March 2, 1982 • This semester I am taking one of my old favorite subjects, history. Sarah is in my class, too. It is a huge lecture class that also has a discussion session run by a teacher's assistant.

Our teaching assistant is Lyn Palermo. Sarah and I got our history papers back. She gave us both Fs. I can't believe it! An F. In history? I've been studying it intensely for years. What was wrong with this paper? I can't believe Sarah got the same grade.

We each are going to make an appointment to go see Ms. Palermo.

March 5, 1982 • Ms. Palermo informed me that my writing is really bad. She suggested that perhaps I should seek some remedial assistance. "Remedial" is the actual word she uses.

Are you crazy? I was thinking. Aloud I said to her, Why would you suggest that? What's wrong with this paper? Please point out what you're talking about.

I found her examples in response to my request minimal and unsatisfactory. No teacher has ever been so condescending to me in my life. I am not one to wear my accomplishments on my sleeve, but for her benefit I tolled them off: National Achievement Scholar, my English scores on the PSAT and SAT, all my extra honors English classes, and the final irony that my mom is, among other course areas, an English teacher.

I don't think so I told her, not this kid, not remedial English. That's fine if you need it, but that's not the problem here, so what is?

"Well," she replied, "whatever you say. If you want to pass this course, you are going to have to ace the final."

After our conference, her face was red. I can only imagine how my face looked.

In essence, she told Sarah the same thing.

We are the only two black people in the class. I'm sorry, I said to Sarah, I've got to give this one to prejudice. I've heard about this particular kind of school nonsense, and this one is too blatant to ignore. Sarah and I have agreed to study intensely for the history final, much harder than we usually study for any other subject.

I don't use this word often, but it fits. Bitch.

This one's for us, Sarah:

A WALK

One day while traveling dreamily and serenely down the road of life
I turned a corner
And what I saw in front of me
Changed me forever
It was something far different
From what I'd seen before
And it stopped me and my illusions in our tracks
It was reality.

All my life, I have never been an intense studier. And I've always done very well (except for a few science and math courses). And I believe I deserved the grades I got in those courses. For this course, I am going to take studying to a whole other level.

July 1, 1982 • We each got a D.

What a coincidence. A D in American history. Right now, I really hate Lyn Palermo. In all my years in school, I've never disliked or felt more incorrectly judged by a teacher than by her.

I am not going to let this D derail me. No way. Not this kid. Not this journey. I've got too much journey left to travel, and too many exciting things ahead to let this screw it up. Nor am I going to let it bum me out.

OK enough. I am moving on to have a great summer.

July 28, 1982 • Chris and I have grown inseparable. Even though he lives in Massachusetts and I in New York, we are managing to spend a good amount of time together over this summer vacation. I've now spent a lot of time with his family, who are pretty cool. I know his mom likes me. I'm not so sure about his dad. His dad is kind of difficult to read. Seems there's a lot of that going around.

I just got back home from visiting with Chris and his family at their Cape Cod summer home. We swam, he taught me how to race his dad's motorboat, we loved, and at times, we argued.

I don't know where to start
Thoughts flow through my mind
And my hand needs to grip the pen
To set them down and record these feelings
So that I can touch and hold them.
Tonight I was moved
You moved me so that I wanted to cry
And smile and hold you all at the same time
To sit and do inconsequential work is unthinkable
I want to savor you and the joy we give each other
Through our arguments and our ecstasy.

Mostly, though, we've been dreaming. We plan to get married after graduation from college. We are going to wait until after we both graduate, but we are clear that we both want to do this. A few of our friends think our relationship is kind of serious for college, but we don't care; we know our own minds.

For my birthday, Chris took me to an outdoor Rick James concert! He bought me this beautiful cultured pearl bracelet, and, above all, he gave—and gives me—his heart full of love.

August 4, 1982 • Back in New York, in between my visits with Chris, I've been spending the summer working and having a blast with my friends. It's like a reunion when we all come home for summers, a chance to catch up in person. The phone works great, though, as my phone bills continue to show. Like with Will Joe, since he didn't have the money to come back to BU this past year, we've kept in touch by phone.

When it comes to work, I've been working for different temporary agencies. My friend Andrea turned me on to them. Andrea's from Queens, too. When she started BU a year after me, family friends told her to look me up. That good ol' community connection. That's how we found each other. She's become part of the crew and a great friend. Anyway, Andrea's older sister turned us on to the world of temporary agencies. If your receptionist and typing skills are good, you can be placed all over the city in different companies, make money, and maintain a flexible schedule. We've both turned out to be naturals.

August 6, 1982 • Justine is pregnant. Her sister, in her infinite wisdom, has put her out. Her boyfriend, James, that she met at college, is being somewhat supportive, but he's having a hard time with the situation. So she's come to stay with us for a while. While we work together to figure things out.

August 10, 1982 • Justine has decided to keep her baby. She, Mommy and I spend many hours talking about what she is going to do to make it work. Together, we watch what we eat, although I can't deal with drinking milk. My friend is a true survivor. I know she is hurt by the actions of her sister, but she doesn't show it. Justine says she is only concerned about her baby and making this work. I think, deep down inside, it feels good for her to have somebody who is truly going to belong to her, and her to him . . . or her. Justine is working temp jobs too, through the agency Andrea and I use. But she's seriously worried about money and how she is going to afford this. Staying with us really helps, and I know the emotional support and love makes a difference. But Justine is scared, too. And I am worried about the fact that soon it will be time for me to go back to school. I can't leave Justine like this.

August 21, 1982 • Justine's older cousin, Rita, has agreed to have Justine live with her at Rita's apartment in New Jersey! Justine is relieved. She doesn't mention her sister anymore. She feels that while living with Rita, and working as long as possible, and with money from James, she can make this work.

Justine is determined to finish college, make a home for her baby, and be happy. I know she will do it. Justine is a fighter.

September 14, 1982 • Sherry is a freshman here at BU! After two years of living in different states, we are together again. I am so thrilled my sister is here at BU. She's made quite an arrival among the upperclassmen.

My sister has grown up to be quite a beauty. Back home, those mean and ignorant kids that used to make fun of her teeth . . . those same guys now stand with their tongues hanging out of their mouths as my beautiful sister walks by. She doesn't care, though. She's not mean or nice to them; she just is. Sherry is very self-sufficient. I always knew my sister was beautiful on the inside and out. Now the rest of the world knows it, too. I love my sister more than anything.

I now live in a full-fledged apartment. I was so excited to land this apartment and move out of Warren Towers, which, God knows, I had grown tired of. Sherry lives in one of the brown-stone dorms on Bay State Road, the same one as Andrea. She and Sherry have become tight as well. Along with Chris and Sarah, and my old friend Lincoln from Jamaica who used to share my glasses (he's in Chris' class), and some other close friends, we have become a family. We lost another friend who didn't come back after last year: Tamara. I see that, at times, college can be a challenging place to stick it out.

I've been thinking a lot lately about what I believe is important in life, the things I value and the dreams I have. Not just about career, but maybe even more important for me, dreams with the people I love. Sherry and I have this dream that when we get older and have families, we are going to create lots of traditions for our families to enjoy and share in. And years from now, even long after we are gone and our grandchildren are old, they'll still be enjoying those traditions we began.

I think we both feel kind of sad that our families on both Mommy and Daddy's sides aren't really close to us. We are thankful for our school family and their families that we have become a part of.

With our dream, we know that we can create for ourselves and our future children whatever it is we want and want them to have.

October 23, 1982 • Today I was hanging out with Sarah at our apartment, cooking some curried chicken that smell so good we could practically hear the reggae music as we stirred.

Sarah, I said, I feel different about school this year. I want to get really serious about my work. I've been thinking a lot about this, and I love the work I have been doing in journalism. I want to figure out what I'm going to do with all that I'm learning. I can't believe we're juniors already, I continued. Time is flying. Before we know it, it will be time to get a real job and really be adults. I thought it was a big deal turning eighteen, but maybe the really big deal will be being out there on our own, without school.

Sarah, lying on my bed with Raggedy Andy on her knee, agreed. "I know what you mean about the future. I've been working really hard all along, and still now, I feel that it is time to get more focused on what I am going to do next. You know I want to travel. Really see the world. And have a beautiful home and be a true career woman. In control of my destiny. I love my major of advertising and marketing. But where do I want to go with it? How's it all going to fit in?"

I nodded my head. I'm not sure, Sarah, but I'll tell you this. I think it's great that you have a lot of your goals and dreams honed out. I've always loved that about you. I guess part of it is that we can plan and take it one day at a time, as well. Tough balancing act, huh? Speaking of balancing acts—I didn't realize it was getting so late. You guys better save me some of that chicken. I am due at the bookstore for the afternoon shift. You know how my boss gets when I am late to get on the cash register.

"I'm glad you love that job, Sha, because you sure spend enough time there," Sarah said. "It's a good thing they don't mind Chris coming in to visit you, or he'd be missing you like crazy."

Yeah, mon, me love my job, and my other tree jobs as well, I said, with a pretty good imitation of the *Saturday Night Live* Jamaican skit about all the jobs each person in the family has.

Seriously though, I do have lots of jobs. That's because I go to the Quickie Job Service (what a funny name for it, hmmm) and get jobs there, too. Last week I had a job experience I'll never forget. I took a job washing dishes. It was for a family that was having a huge celebration.

I found the house, a lovely home in Brookline. The family showed me into the children's room, where I sat with the little kids who were playing, waiting to be summoned in to do my job. Eventually I was called into the kitchen and put to work. All the food looked mouthwatering as each course was whisked out of the kitchen on lovely platters. I was instructed as to where the dishes and crystal were kept and given rubber gloves. Starving, I began my tasks, plunging my hands into a sink of soapy water and dirty dishes.

I cleaned many dishes, serving platters, and pieces of cookware that day. It took about four hours. The family was polite to me, and one of the children smiled at me, but it was hard work. Not so much the scrubbing, but how I felt inside.

When I finished my work, shortly before sundown, I was paid, told thank you, and let out the front door. Walking down the narrow, tree-lined sidewalk, hungry and tired, I felt my spirit lighten with each step I took away from the house. I began to run toward the trolley station, even though I wasn't late for anything.

I had a sense of pain, appreciation for those who had to do that work every day, and a sense of freedom as I jumped on the trolley headed back to my life as a student and the homework I completed with unusual zeal that night.

December 2, 1982 • Recently, the wonderful poet Nikki Giovanni came to Boston. We took the trolley to go hear her speak. The place was packed with people, but I managed to get close enough eventually to get her autograph. Imagine writing poetry that you can share with everyone, where people are so touched by your words that they gather together to hear you . . . and leave feeling the better because of it. What a wonderful dream.

March 16, 1983 • This semester with my courses I've had the opportunity to study and write about many of the things going on in this world. The more I study and then write up news stories that we broadcast in our simulated newsroom, the more I realize that, while I enjoy this work tremendously and feel like a natural at it, I want to do more. I don't know if the right word is really more, so much as making my contribution in a different way. I tell about what happens in the news, and I know by doing that I can empower people through knowledge. But what if I were part of making the news? As in, *doing work* to change and improve people's lives? I have to keep thinking about this.

May 4, 1983 • I bought my first big purchase with some of the money I've saved from my job: my own little television set. It's beautiful, and it took me forever to pick it out. Chris came with me, and we brought it home and hooked it right up. I'd like to get a car, but I know that I am a far cry from being able to afford one. One of these days that will happen, but it's going to be a while. Meantime, the trolley works just fine. And it is great that Chris has a little car that he piles us all into for excursions out of the city.

May 7, 1983 • Sherry's birthday. We do our crew tradition of throwing a surprise party for the birthday person. I like to think of a way to make it really tricky, and to make sure that each person's birthday party fits who they are. The mystery questions always are the how, what, and when of it. Sherry is great at guessing. But we got her. We planned her party outside, along the Charles River. It was a great one. We tricked her even better than we did Sarah last week for her party.

After Sherry's party, she and I hung out in her dorm room. Sherry is loving BU. She is taking all premed classes, but she's finding she doesn't like them as much as she though she would.

"I'm just not happy with this course of study," she confided. "I don't think it's what I want to do with my life. Even though I've studied premed these past years and interned in a hospital under a doctor you know I admired, I just am not feeling like this is right for me."

Sherry, you've been thinking about this for quite a while. You've got a great head on your shoulders. You always have, I replied. (We both laughed when I said it. It's so true.) Anyway, I think you are right to reconsider medicine, if it's not calling to you. That makes sense to me, if you're not happy in it. It sounds like you're pretty sure about where you are at. Why go further down a road, if you know it isn't your path? I think Mommy gets it, but she's a little disappointed. But I figure you gotta do what you gotta do.

May 10, 1983 • The semester is almost over. I'll be a senior in September.

Conversations these days center a lot around what we are going to do after graduation. I've been thinking about it. I love my broadcast journalism major and the work I am doing in school.

Alicia and I still talk some, although, being a senior this year, she hasn't had much time to hang. She is planning to attend law school and is anxiously awaiting news from the schools she has applied to.

I, too, have been thinking strongly about law school. I find the idea of going to law school intrigues me, though I've canceled out some of my other choices, like being a dancer or a model. I've dabbled in both, but I don't want to spread myself too, too thin. I'm narrowing things down. I've traveled a ways since freshman year. I am still going to do a lot of singing . . . and dance for a hobby . . . and write. Always writing. But next step career-wise, that's what it's time to determine. Well, as Mommy used to say, we'll see.

Lately though, Mommy has stopped saying "we'll see" and just goes for it with what she decides at the time. Just as Sherry and I have been encouraging her to do for years.

June 13, 1983 • Sarah, Andrea and I are working in Boston for the summer. We all got internships!

The three of us found this scummy little apartment in Brookline where we threw this old dusty rug out the back window our first night and woke up killing roaches. The good news is, we can afford it.

My internship is with WCVB-TV, the Boston ABC affiliate. It was pretty competitive to get it. I almost didn't go on the interview because I had a horribly sore throat. Basically one step from laryngitis. The thing was I thought back to when I did my monologue in Kentucky with strep throat; I figured, if I can get through that, I could make it through this. So I went on the interview. There were five people interviewing me. I guess they understood what I was saying, as well as recognizing my commitment and enthusiasm to do positive work to have an influence on the community. I got the job.

I've been assigned to *City Streets*, a black community news and feature show.

July 1, 1983 • *City Streets* is run by a really handsome (perpetual?) bachelor, George Masters. He gets a lot of calls from sexy-sounding women. However, taking messages is a very small part of my job.

George allows me to do work that has a lot more responsibility than what most interns get to do. He even lets me handle directing the editing of footage. I love every minute of my work here. I get to generate story ideas, research news and feature stories, and accompany George for important interviews. I think George kind of has a sink-or-swim philosophy. Since my first day, he has expected me to jump into the deep water. And he never asked if I could swim.

That's OK. I've discovered I like this form of instruction. I am swimming in water that appears bottomless. My days are very exciting.

At home, I talk about my work with George all the time. I think

Chris gets jealous. But it's just that I love my job, and I get a kick out of George's lifestyle. It's entertaining.

July 15, 1983 • I am producing my own segment for *City Streets*. The ultimate opportunity. I can't believe it. It will air on the show and actually say, "Written and produced by Sharon Simpson."

My segment is called "The Children of Biracial Parentage." It seems to me that there are articles and books about interracial marriages and a lot of history on the subject, but not as much focus upon the unique issues that face children of biracial parentage. George agrees with me and is allowing me to do this story.

I was even able to interview Dr. Alvin Poussaint, a renowned psychologist, on the subject. He was extremely helpful.

I also interviewed several biracial people. Chris was one of them. He was great. I was proud of him. I feel really proud of myself, too. This is the most challenging and exciting job I've ever had.

August 5, 1983 • For the second half of the summer, I've been assigned to work with *Chronicle*, an evening news program. Here I'm seeing a bustling nightly program in action. There are several producers who are constantly developing stories. They are always on the lookout for a story.

August 10, 1983 • I can't believe it.

Today was the most incredible day. The way it happened was an odd blend of serendipity, fate, and nausea . . . not in that order.

A really nice producer, Amanda, took me on a shoot with her. But not just any shoot. It was to interview this hot new group, the New Edition.

I've done a lot of the research for her for the interview and, of course, I really love the New Edition's song "Candy Girl," so how excited was I to get this opportunity.

We drove in the Channel 5 van, picking up the camera-woman and audio man on the way. But then Amanda started feeling really queasy.

Finally she told Jim, the audio guy to pull over. She actually got out of the van, went to the side of the road, and threw up.

The three of us sat in the van looking at each other, worried. "I'll be all right," Amanda kept saying. But she looked terrible.

"Amanda," Jim said. "You need to go home and get to bed. You can't do this."

"We've scheduled this interview and the kids [the guys are all only 14 and 15 years old] are leaving for Europe. This is it. By the time they get back from Europe, they're going to be even hotter, and we will have missed our exclusive."

That's when they all looked at me.

"You can do it, Sharon," Amanda said encouragly, in between looking like she was about to barf again.

"Just stick to interviewing them about their trip to Europe and stardom."

Oh my God, I thought, summoning up all my courage. Outside, I said. "OK, Amanda, I'll do my best."

Jim and Anita, the camerawoman, and I went out to lunch, with them encouraging me all the way and giving me tips and pointers. I was so nervous, but I knew it was a fantastic opportunity. If I can just get through this day, I thought, and do it well. I can't wait to tell Sarah and Andrea this one tonight.

Their studio was in a house, a huge kind of ramshackle structure in Dorchester. Their manager, Maurice Star, already well-known for others he's managed, greeted us, as did many folks in the neighborhood when they saw the television van pull up.

Then we met the New Edition. They all had on warm-up suits and gold. Except one of the guys, Bobby Brown, had on all silver and a friendly and rather big ego. I had forgotten they were so young, only 14 and 15 years old. They were enthusiastic and made my job of interviewing surprisingly smooth and fun. It seemed like this was new for them, as well. We shot the interview on the roof, since it afforded the most light.

Not only did I interview them on their European debut, but they also let me film them rehearsing "Candy Girl" and "Popcorn Love" as well. So we got even more footage than Amanda had anticipated. At the finish, I felt this huge sense of joy and relief. When I left, they even invited me to the huge celebration scheduled to happen on their return. I told Sarah and Andrea, you know I'm not missing that!

September 14, 1983 • It was an awesome summer, work-wise. I wish I could say the same for Chris and me, but it seems that the tension between us is growing. Before, we'd only argue once in a while. When we argued, we argued big. But the makeups were big, too. Now, however, it seems that we disagree more and more and have less and less patience with each other and our points of view. We argue over dumb little stuff, like didn't he tell me before he likes Coke better than Pepsi, and why don't I remember that? And big stuff, like my thinking it matters to get involved in the debate about black student politics, and him thinking it's not as important, that we should focus more on ourselves.

I just feel more serious about life, and I have lots of thoughts on my mind. It doesn't feel as though our relationship can stay the way it's been. Life is moving so quickly these days. But it feels as if we are kind of stuck. Maybe part of it is that I am graduating this May and Chris has one more year to go, so my head is in a different space. I don't know.

I love Chris, I really do. I just know I don't feel as close to him as before. I'm scared to admit that to him. I guess I've been scared to admit it to myself. And I don't know what to do about it.

I CLOSE MY MIND TO ALL BUT AIR
I seek to have no thoughts
In this way I find I can bear
This limbo I have wrought
Loneliness is a hollow word
That tends to give one pain
When hurt imbeds within one's heart
And strength one tries to feign.
My spirit strives for inner peace
And clearness of my mind
But pain you can inflict in me
Makes it so hard to find.

September 22, 1983 • I was invited back by WCVB to work on a second internship this fall. That's an honor, because interns are seldom invited back due to the large number of students competing to work at the station. I work in the Public Affairs Division, working on housing, education and a myriad of other issues that I believe really matter in strengthening the public's awareness and improving the circumstances of many people in the community. Ultimately, I believe I am learning more about the ways in which I can help people through sharing knowledge. (We won't talk about the fact that my first day on the job, I got in an accident in my boss' car when I went to pick up her lunch.) Ugh.

November 15, 1983 • This year I have the most amazing course, a sociology course with Professor Howard Zinn. We are reading a book by a famous anarchist from the 1920s, Emma Goldman's *Living My Life*. These days I am driving everybody crazy by constantly quoting Emma Goldman and loving her story. It's making me really examine what I think about laws and their purpose for us as a society. While I don't agree with anarchy as a means to solve our nation's problems, I admire Emma Goldman's commitment to equality, to women's rights, and to the power that we each have as individuals to contribute to society. Emma had a vision for this nation, and she fought her whole life to make it happen.

I have been thinking harder about my own visions of how I could make a difference in this world.

December 4, 1983 • Sherry's boyfriend, Patrick, whom she's been seeing since her senior year of high school, transferred to BU so they could be together. He has become part of the crew.

Sherry and I and most of our crew have now been singing with Inner Strength, BU's gospel choir, for the past two years. I have begun to think more about my spirituality, as in taking my own responsibility for it, not as a child whose parents send her to church, but as a young woman, looking into my own heart.

At the concert last night, the funniest thing happened. It was one of those Sharon and Sherry twin experiences. We stood in the soprano section (I'm singing soprano now instead of alto), singing our hearts out. Sherry was standing directly in front of me. The director was directing a particularly challenging part of the song, one of those parts where you continuously stop and then start singing, and then hold the note, and then utter silence. Somehow I knew Sherry didn't know to cease singing at the utter silence part. Right at the moment when the whole choir was about to go silent, I subtly kicked her and she got it. She closed her mouth just as she was about to raise her voice in song.

"How'd you know?" everybody asked later, when we, laughing, told the story. Sherry and I just smiled, "We've always been like this."

December 6, 1983 • Chris and I aren't getting along. I love him so much, and I know he loves me. It just feels as though there is less and less for us to talk about. It hurts. And I find myself getting mad at him, even though I don't know why. He says, "What's wrong with you, Sharon?" I can't answer the question.

December 8, 1983 • Spike Lee, a young, black film director, came to speak to our black communications organization, Third World Expressions, at the MLK Center on campus. He showed us a movie he made for graduate school, *Joe's Bed-Stuy Barbershop: We Cut Heads.*

It was good. After the movie he talked about his experiences and goals. He's going to make movies with powerful messages. He's got a lot to say. Seems as if he's got a good amount of courage, talent and attitude, capital A. Yes, he's somebody really out there, pursuing his dream.

December 20, 1983 • Christopher and I broke up.

It's been so long
Since I wrote you a song
Or a story or a poem
Perhaps all the music has left me
In my desperation to seek a harmonious existence
The tune within
Has mellowed to a whisper

February 23, 1984 • Even though Chris and I are now apart, our whole gang is still together. After all, we are each other's family. And Chris and my breakup does not change that.

We are all a family.
Our gang
That's how we live.
It's hard, though. I have gone out on some dates with other

guys, but I am still hurting over my parting from Chris, even though I know it was the right thing to do. Chris is dating other girls, too. And it pains me to see it. We have grown in different directions. It breaks my heart to say it, but I know we are not what we once were together. I don't see our future together anymore. We are on separate journeys. Still, it is so hard to accept this insight and to live it. It is even more difficult for Chris to see it, but I know in my heart it is so. Sometimes I feel scared to continue my journey without him, but there is this part of me that is excited, too.

March 1, 1984 • I've thought a lot about what I want to do with my future. I have decided I definitely want to go to law school. I can learn a lot more about the law and the ways in which it can be used to make a positive difference. The ideas of justice and equality are important to me, but I am not always sure how to envision making them happen for all people. I do believe, though, that there is plenty of work to be done. Maybe law school can help get me on that road.

Also, while college has been a blast, it hasn't been a truly tough academic challenge. I know in part that is because of who I have been in the matter. But I want to really challenge myself mentally, and I believe law school will certainly do that. I plan to take a year between graduation and law school, to work, get some communications experience and get myself ready for law school.

Sarah and I have decided that we are ready for a new adventure. So we are going to look for jobs in Washington, D.C., and move there after a summer of saving up money and . . . we hope . . . finding jobs. Daddy is going to help us move our things down there, which is pretty cool.

They say it is really hard to find jobs in our field of communications in a big city like DC, but I don't want to go to some little town in the middle of nowhere to begin this part of my journey. So, as always, I am taking my chances and not worrying about what "they say." DC, here we come.

April 12, 1984 • Lately our crew spends a lot of time talking about what we think is going on in the world. Much of what we talk about is our feelings about relationships and values on campus, especially within the black community.

Really this is a time when I see us beginning to express ourselves, not just with each other, but with the world around us. We've decided to take a stand, not only by how we chose to live with our beliefs, but by what we have to share with others.

April 15, 1984 • We gathered together in Sherry's room, we girls, and talked. Finally, we decided that for Umoja, the black student union's performance night, we would write and perform an original play, and offer our own powerful message.

"Let's not hold back our feelings," Sherry said. "If we don't take a stand and be really honest about what we think is up with us, as black people on this campus, and how to encourage us all, I don't think there's a point to our doing this."

We all agreed that we have to really go for the gusto in what we have to say.

Basically, what we are feeling is that black folks on this campus spend too much time at odds with each other and not enough time encouraging and appreciating each other. We are tired of folks snapping on each other, being caught up in what's accepted, what's cool, and what's in. We believe that we all need to look beyond these elements to uncover and not be afraid to share who we really are, whether that fits in or not.

So we wrote *The Mask*, to pass on an ultimate message of unity.

May 5, 1984 • The play was performed with us all wearing the same black masks. As each one of us makes the choice to share our real feelings and have the courage to be ourselves with all of our strengths and vulnerabilities, we find the spirit to remove the mask and reveal who we really are.

Performing *The Mask* while a month shy of graduation is a form of graduation in itself. I believe it is a rite of passage for all of us. We have taken a stand, stood up in front of all, and shared our beliefs and our vision of how we could all be together.

It is a feeling I will not soon forget, and an encouragement for me to continue on this road.

It seems we come so far each day
The road of life is long
And traveling on an untried path
We make our steps a song
For those who walk to a silent beat
The road is infinite
But music adds wings to our feet
A tune we can't forget.

Pack Vision

PACK VISION. THAT GLORIOUS STATE WHERE dreams and reality can merge. When we believe.

As I've grown older, I've learned how essential Vision is to my journey. Having the Vision to dream and set goals for myself. To bring Vision to what I do . . . to my plans for the future, goals, dreams, ideas, images . . . Vision. Even when my dreams change or evolve or falter, maintaining Vision in my life makes the difference between my charting a course and simply wandering. And oftentimes, to my successful arrival at a juncture or goal I have set.

Vision is what keeps me going even when the terrain up ahead is foggy or unclear. I know the direction in which I am headed, I know my goal, and I am committed to traveling the distance to get there.

I was soon to be reminded however, that while Vision is invaluable, Visions may turn out very differently than we plan them.

6

Slave Dance

Washington, D.C.

March 5, 1985 • Late night, Saturday in DC, and almost a week has passed since I talked to him.

Sarah and I had walked to the 7-Eleven on the corner of 14th and Rhode Island, the unsafe end of the street. Coming out of the store, we bumped into him, going in. We stood on the corner, almost a face-off. I can't believe it is what it is. I am pregnant.

Sarah stood back, allowing us space to talk, yet somehow still completing the circle.

I always know he'll tell me the truth even when it's painful or it would be easier for him to lie. Like just saying "I love you."

Did you call me? I asked him. Have you tried to reach me at all this week?

It would have been easy for him to say yes. It would also not have been the truth. "No, I didn't," he said, looking me straight in the eye.

I see, I said, equally direct. Good night.

Sarah and I walked back upstairs to our one-bedroom (when you closed the sliding door) apartment. Lying on my futon next to Sarah's futon, with *Saturday Night Live* blaring on the television, I thought to myself: I am on my own. That old expression, "I've got to pull my own little red wagon," came to mind.

I felt numb.

The phone rang.

It's him. He wants to talk.

We walked for hours through DC. Ending up on the mall with the beautiful Washington Monument in the distance. I was struck by the beauty of the night and the ugliness of our situation. I remembered another time, in the sunlight, when we lay on this same smooth green grass, not far from where we were now sitting.

As I looked at his profile, hearing his words but not making much sense of them, I was again struck by his long eyelashes, and I thought how the baby might have them too.

He said he's not ready to be a father. I know that.

I'm scared to be a mother.

But I love this baby. And I keep dreaming in my mind how I can make this work.

March 6, 1985 • I love you, Knight Houma, I keep saying in my head. But I don't say it out loud. Ever since we met last spring when I came here for that minority communications conference, there's been this powerful connection between us.

He had moved here to DC the year before, through his job. Knight's a pilot. Even though it's a cliché, he is very much the strong, silent type, a Samoan from Hawaii. We found ourselves with a connection that transcended our different personalities and experiences. We hit it off right away and kept in touch.

When I moved to Washington, we started seeing each other. At first it was just friendship, fun, and excitement. But as the months progressed, I found myself falling in love with him, though his feelings don't seem clear. This relationship is very unlike my relationship with Chris. Chris was my boyfriend and the only man I ever thought I'd be with. When we broke up, it was so impossible to imagine sleeping with anyone else.

Now here Knight and I are, friends and lovers. Knight, always so sexy, so passionate in his approach to everything, his work—his goals—and his lovemaking. He loves our friendship, our bond. A totally new type of relationship for me.

I'd kept thinking it would change and grow into the kind of love I knew we could share, do share deep down inside. Even though I want more, to be truly committed to each other, I've been unable to express it, or to walk away and just be friends. So I stayed. And now it's too late.

MIND SURRENDER

She,
Who always had so much to say
Suddenly lost her voice to a vortex of feeling
Words were submerged in a crescendo of sensation
Louder than she had ever spoken before
She heard her heart screaming in her breast
Emotion overwhelmed her
Threatening to rise up and choke the very life from her soul
She struggles to breathe and keep her previously concise mind clear.
Until she sees that surrender is the only method for her survival.
"I love you," she is forced to whisper
Setting her heart free
And forever chaining her mind.

Here I am, pregnant. Taking stupid chances without being responsible, either of us. The irony is I'd gone to the gynecologist earlier this month and gotten birth control pills to start taking at the end of my next period. Only my next period didn't come.

I guess I had fantasized that one day he would not wrestle with his feelings for me, but would realize how much he loved me, as I do him. Now, I see that isn't going to happen. If ever there was a moment to determine our feelings, it's now. From the way he is acting, it's clear to me that loving me, truly being in love with me, is far from his mind. So I have to accept that, along with the pregnancy.

March 13, 1985 • Sitting here at work, at the Insurance Institute for Highway Safety's Communications Department. The Institute is located in the famed Watergate building. That part of the job is exciting. But it's the only part that is. This is the most boring job I have ever had in my life. The famous "they" who said it's hard to find a communications job in a big city, straight out of school, weren't kidding. I sent resumes and resume tapes to many places in DC. I was told that at this job I'd have the chance to work with the public, the media, and the government. It had sounded exciting and like a good place to start while I studied for the LSATs, as the law school entrance exams are called, and applied to law schools.

I couldn't have been more wrong. The reality of this job is quite different. I have been so disappointed with it in the past few months of working here. My supervisor spoon-feeds me every small responsibility, like how to properly stuff an envelope (I'm not kidding). Not at all like George Masters, who threw me straight into the deep water, the way I like it.

Oh, well, right now the slow nature of this job suits me. Because I am feeling so sick. I make several trips to the bathroom a day. Some of them include kneeling in front of the toilet bowl. I try to hide how sick I feel from my buddies here at work.

Today is Wednesday; when I got off work I rushed to the train to travel to my second job, waitressing at a really nice seafood restaurant, Charley's Crab. It's my first waitress job. I always wanted to be a waitress and wear a uniform. I love my waitress job. Getting this job included a week's worth of training that culminated in a written exam. You had to know things like what garnish goes with what entrée and what size plate it would be served on, as well as practically acquire a bartender's knowledge of mixed drinks and whether a lemon, olive, lime, or mint is the appropriate accompaniment. I loved it, and I got a 98 on the test!

The past several months there have been great. But tonight I felt sick as a dog. My friend Ken, a cook, teased me, "You act like you're pregnant or something." If only he knew.

I made it through the night. Now I am at home and can rest.

March 25, 1985 • Knight was in the shower. I'd had to humble myself to ask if I could stay the night. He didn't ask me, even though we had to be at the clinic really early. I was reading the brochure and instructions. All of a sudden, I realized that the whole visit doesn't take an hour and a half; it is the procedure itself that does. I told him an hour and a half for the whole visit, and that is what he had budgeted for the day. I sneaked to the telephone and called Sarah. It was still early enough that she hadn't left for work yet. She told me again that she would drop everything and come with me if I wanted her to, but I told her to go on to work. I'd be OK.

When he came out, I found the courage to tell him my mistake. He said, "I guess I'll just have to leave the clinic early to get to work."

In the waiting room, with lots of different folks in various stages of emotions, he was making jokes that I didn't really think were funny, but I smiled, because.

In for quick counseling.
Back out to wait again.
It's almost time for him to leave.
For me to go in.

I don't want him to go.
But I have learned to control myself in so many areas of life.
So I wait inevitably for them to summon me inside and for
him to leave.
By myself.
Except really I have been all along.
Except for the baby.
Sleep. And I don't feel anything.
Except emotions that I don't have language to describe.
Coming to isn't easy.
And somehow my blood pressure has gotten really low.
So that I am forced to stay there an extra long time.
Finally, I am allowed to leave.
Weak but in one piece, depending on how you look at it.
Outside it has begun to snow.

I have thought about walking home, but I know I will never make it. So I catch a taxi.

I stop and buy my favorite Swanson turkey TV dinner and a box of brownies to bake, comfort food from my growing-up years. Maybe I'll eat it later. Right now I'm not hungry.

If I can just make it home and to the bed.

INSIDE AND OUT
While you were out.
I continued to love.
You.
You didn't care
That your baby was inside
Me.
When you came home
And the baby was gone

You left too
Now I am empty
Inside and out.

March 26, 1985 • Knight, Sarah and I sat at our folding dining room table, looking out into the stars. I sat on Knight's lap as the three of us talked about nothing. The cramps were bad. Though I said nothing about the pain, I drew comfort from my contact with Knight, his hand resting on my back. And from knowing that when Knight left, Sarah would help me heat towels to place on my stomach, until I could fall asleep. And get up for work tomorrow.

March 27, 1985 • Around the same time I've been living all this, I got a letter from Stanford Law School. I've been staring at it for a while now. So far, I've only applied to Georgetown, where I thought I really wanted to go. Stay here in DC, figuring I'd head out to California after law school, since it is still calling to me so strongly. After my LSAT scores came in so high, I started getting a lot of letters, and I received the recruitment letter from Stanford.

I decided to call. I was feeling bold, in go-for-it mode, what did I have to lose? The dean of students was away from her desk, and I thought, oh well, so much for this. I probably won't bother to call back. I continue to talk to her assistant, a really nice lady whose daughter lives in DC, I discovered, as we enjoyed chatting further. In fact, we chatted so long that the dean returned, and I ended up talking with her.

Maybe some moments truly can change our lives forever.

I've decided to apply. Even though it is the last minute, and even though the pain of these cramps is still excruciating. It is something to shoot for. Something good that could actually happen.

March 29, 1985 • I wrote the application in severe pain, from my stomach to my heart. But I kept typing because I know it is my future, and if I stop now, what has been the point?

March 30, 1985 • The Stanford Law School dean of students came to DC. She invited me to join the dinner she had arranged for students already admitted to SLS. I accepted, though the pain and cramps continued to be severe.

The dean was a beautiful, sophisticated black woman, impressively professional and gracious at the same time. I admired her greatly. Despite the wealth of emotions that were inside of me, I pushed myself to be present in mind and spirit.

At the dinner I sat curling my toes in pain, as I earnestly talked about the merits of SLS. And I prayed to God that I can go there in the fall, so that there is, at least, some point to it all.

April 15, 1985 • Knight came over tonight. He told Sarah and me that he is moving. He has gotten a better job in Arizona. He is not sorry to go. He hates DC. I play my favorite song, "Hard Habit to Break." Knight used to get so tired of hearing me play it over and over that he threatened to break the forty-five record. At the time, the irony of the song escaped me; now, with every spin of the record, the words resound in my ears: *"I guess I thought you'd be here forever, another illusion I chose to create . . ."*

May 14, 1985 • Knight's gone.
But once again, my poetry never fails me.

Positive.
She said.
And looked me straight in the eye.
I nodded my head once, perhaps a little jerkily.

You knew?

She asked.

Yes.

I nodded my head once again.

An almost imperceptible twist to my lips

Do you know what you want to do?

No.

Call us.

Sure. Thanks.

Walking out.

Different and yet the same.

Sure I knew.

Now I know for sure.

Positive.

I said.

And looked him straight in the eye.

Insertion of breath

Long drawn-out sigh

The unbelievable is to be believed.

There between you and me

Intimately resting between us lies a baby

Safe

For now

Do you know what you want to do?

No.

Yes.

What does it matter?

What I want.

That is not part of the choice

Choice?

Poor choice of words.

A baby safe for now

You don't see it that way
You don't see a baby
Choice
Let's go
Money
Sure
Two hours
Well, an hour and a half
Time enough
To solve the problem
Problem
No
Not anymore
Not for you
Anyway
Now?
Hey, sure.
I go on.
No problem
Outside
Anyway
Positive?
Sure.
After all, negative never entered into the situation.

July 1, 1985 • I don't know if I am writing today to keep myself awake at work . . . or from an honest desire to make mention of life. Here I am at my long-term temp job at a lobbying office because I couldn't take it anymore at the Insurance Institute and I resigned. It's been several months since I have written anything.

I've been wait-listed for Stanford. The school tells me this is quite an accomplishment, since I applied right at the deadline for applications. Nonetheless, wait-listing means that I have to wait to see if a spot will open up for me to attend. I've made plans to move my things back to New York at the end of the summer in preparation for going to law school. I figure if I don't get in, I'll stay in New York, live at home for the year, work and save up money and apply again. But I am holding on firmly to the belief that come September, I'll be at Stanford. Sarah has decided to remain in DC. We don't look forward to our parting. I want to have as much fun as possible before it's time to leave. Focus upon having a good time!

July 2, 1985 • "This is why I'm single," seems to be the theme of my life these past few weeks. This last weekend was great. Saturday night, Sarah and I went to Charley's Crab for dinner and, after getting a free glass of wine and strawberry daiquiri and a great Lobster Larry, Sarah and I were pleasantly bombed. We ended up going with Phil and Ken, my buddies who work at Charley's, to a fun gay club, Trax, where I had the best time partying since I got to DC. I danced with Ken all night, and the music was great. I felt I could be really free dancing there and with him. He is definitely crazy, one of our new top prerequisites to what a man has to be. No one too weighty and serious. Although I don't know how Ken would deal with my nuttiness. We didn't leave the club until after 4 A.M.

Then we drove around DC, which is really beautiful at night, and we stopped at a fountain to play, act crazy, and throw water on each other. After that, we went to the Giant supermarket where Phil and Ken bought food, and we came back to our apartment and cooked breakfast. They didn't leave until 7:30 A.M. when Sarah and I crashed into bed.

After we woke up, we went to Lisa's (Sarah's friend from work) for a great dinner. Then I rushed back to meet Ken to go to the movies and see *St. Elmo's Fire*, about seven friends who just graduated. It was really good, but it also kind of depressed me. Ken bought me four roses, and then we came back home.

Sarah was asleep in the "bedroom," if you can call it that, and Ken and I were in the living room. We listened to great music, talked a lot, and then Ken asked me if I wanted to dance. He is a romantic. So there we were, slow dancing in the living room, and it felt comfortable. Right before he was going to leave we began kissing, and that just started the whole thing. I just wish I could either relax and really go with the flow (as they say) or forget trying. Last night went pretty far, and it felt good, but of course I knew I couldn't go all the way, and does that make a difference? I don't know. Am I turning into a tease? It doesn't seem as though I know much of anything anymore.

The only real fucked-up mishap to the evening was when, in heavily making out, my extension braid came out in his hand. (God, that is embarrassing to even write, let alone think about.) I can't wait till that shit is in my past and just another funny story. I'm sure it is for Ken right now. Funny, it seems so long ago that I said cursing wasn't me. And now, here I am using pro-fan-i-ty. Hmm. And not apologizing for it. I guess that's where I am at right now. Even though I think some aspects of me are never going to change—they do . . . Well, telling it like it is . . . I do. And some things about my life that I may hope and pray will change, that I don't have control over . . . don't. Change, that is.

Then we come to Andrew and me. Ironically, I met him at Knight's going-away party. He's from Tennessee originally and is a friend of Knight's brother and extremely fine, maybe even the finest man I've ever gone out with (including Knight). Andrew came over and flirted with me, and boy, did I flirt back. Back in the day, Crystal would have been proud. I guess I was really trashed. That's what Knight said later. He seemed pretty angry at me, even though *he's* been clear we are only friends.

Andrew talks about how much he likes me and wants me, and I am confused because I guess I find it so hard to believe. Not that I'm so down on myself or anything, but I guess after feeling so un-special with Knight, it's just difficult to believe I am special to anyone. Except Mario, from Charley's. Another Mario; this one wears gray and pink to meet me for lunch because he knows those are my favorite colors.

But this confusion over men in my life is supposed to be pleasant, which, I guess it would be if it weren't for the fact that my damn braid fell out. Oh, well. Fuck that.

So what am I all about anyway, huh? Let me just shut up and feel good. I bet Ken is going to tell Phil that story. Bummer. That was my word for June. May was "pointless." July is "motherfucker." I am really going to miss a lot of folks here in DC when I leave. But it's nice to know I'll be missed, too. If there is one thing I have definitely learned, it is that you can't predict the future or with whom you will spend it. Now, though, just when I am getting comfortable and settled, it's time to go. I can't wait to get settled in life. It's tough being young. That's for goddamn sure. Ken is only eighteen years old. I am three years older than he. Me, SS, robbing the cradle? Hey, it's not the chronological years that count. Whatever.

It's good to be loved. Sharon.

P.S. I miss my baby. I want it back. Can't happen, so let's forget for now.

July 3, 1985 • Boy, I must be on a writing roll. This is a very emotional year. I hope in retrospect I can clearly recall my feelings, because I don't know if I will do that good a job of writing about them. I can't believe I am going to be twenty-two years old!

As time moves on, I desperately want to go to Stanford! I want to get in so bad. If I don't, I don't know what I will do (mentally, not logistically). Logistically, I'll find a good job in New York. But that's not really what I want. Even though the idea of going to school in California is scary, it's still what I want more than anything.

If I don't go to law school, I'm back at square one. Oh please, God, let me go. Otherwise, it feels like everything is in vain. Time, money, agonizing, and conversation. What will I do? Maybe I could even have had my baby, somehow made a go of it by myself. That seemed so impossible before. But I want my baby desperately, and I can't ever have him (or her) again because I sent him away.

And Knight doesn't understand how I feel, or care, for that matter and that hurts me deeply. Here I am . . . in DC . . . am I trying to live it up or what? Andrew? Ken? Do I want to go for it, or will I only hurt myself in the long run? Which is the answer? What do I want? Never to take a chance again, that's for damn sure. Not unless it's what I want. I think if I don't go to law school, I will end up needing to see a psychiatrist. I need help, someone to hold my hand. I wish what? Marriage? No, it wouldn't have worked. Not without true love. Chris? Hurts, can't seem to fully put it in the past. Please! Help. Take my hand, Lord. I am desperately in need of guidance.

July 9, 1985 • It seems my spirits are better today than at the writing of the last entry. Big ups and downs, that seems to be the order of the day (year). Mommy came and spent several days, and we had a fantastic time together when I wasn't being snappy, which I hate about myself when I act that way with her, but sometimes can't help. She wrote something really beautiful in my "Folio" (high school yearbook). It made me feel really good but also as though I have a lot to live up to. I want to make Mommy proud and be able to do things for her. I was glad I didn't tell her about the abortion. Why put her through that?

Today Mario sent me roses and a beautiful love poem that really touched me. But what can I say? I know how you feel? No, of course not! Life is such an unfair, unequalizing quantity. But at least I have been honest with Mario and not left him hanging.

I'm looking forward to going to the zoo with Ken. I've just got to do things every night. I can't let the time go by me! And I don't want time to think. It's so hard to figure out life.

I did make a decision though . . . Nobody is getting me. Seventeen more days before I move. What the hell is life for, anyway? I'm tired of hurt. Joy hurts, too. OK, so we're human. No choice then. Poor choice of words.

July 10, 1985 • Sherry got accepted to the London Economics Internship Program for her senior year. I think that is fantastic and really hope she goes. It would be the ultimate for her to be there and me at Stanford Law School. I wouldn't blame Mommy then if she told the whole world. Sherry and Patrick are doing great. It's part of what is hard for her about going. Maybe they'll even get married in the next few years. That would be amazing. Lord, we are getting up there in age.

This evening I'm supposed to be going to the zoo or movies with Ken. Friday, Andrea is coming down from New York to visit. So it's a busy schedule. Then next Tuesday is lunch with Lisa from Sarah's job, and Tuesday evening we'll try to hang out with Bill, also from Sarah's job. Then I guess I'll see Andrew whatever evening he has off. Talk about perpetually busy. Too bad right now, I am so damn tired.

July 11, 1985 • Roses Tuesday, a stuffed panda Wednesday from Ken. He won it for me at a carnival. My first stuffed animal ever from a man, at age twenty-one. I've waited so long.

I am so continuously sleepy, it's just not even funny. It's really time to start getting my shit together. Buy a new small notebook for my next experience? I don't know. Not much of anything. A new poem? Unfortunately, I can't remember what it is I felt such an urgent desire to talk about in this entry. Oh, well. Maybe next time.

I remember! I wanted to promise myself that if I go to law school, I will work to the best of my abilities. I will try to tap all areas of my mind as I have never done before. I want to bust it out. No room for fun and good times anymore. No putting off homework and studying until the day before the test. I will go for it and really push.

July 12, 1985 • I am definitely going to miss DC. Most especially some of the very precious friendships I have made here. Sarah and I have become incredibly good friends with this couple, Kathy and Rowena. They have this beautiful, loving home where we spend a lot of time and get fed great meals. They are older than us and think we are crazy and need taking care of since we eat Mrs. Fields cookies for dinner quite often. Hanging with them and learning the details of their relationship and what it's like being gay black women in DC is new to me. In addition to Sarah and my excursions around the city, and seeing Ken and Andrew, time spent with Kathy and Rowena brightens my days considerably.

July 18, 1985 • I found out I didn't get into Georgetown. But by now, I didn't want to go there anyway. It's Stanford for me. I'm holding onto that hope. And, the time draws closer when I must leave DC. "Must" being the operative word. What a life. Try as I might to hold on to things, they just keep slipping away, friends and places I hold near and dear. Still I must leave. What a bummer (I've got to stop using that word). But, as Sarah said, it would be hard to leave in September or January or whenever. So . . . here I go. But to what? Do I wish I had the "strength" to kill myself? Please let me go to law school, or losing my baby will have been for naught. What a reason; I know. Hey, what can I say? I'm having a good-ass time before departing, though. So good I hate to leave, but what choice have I got? It's time to forsake the good time, for the future. Good time? What sense am I making, or is life making, for that matter?

September 5, 1985 • "Have a good day." Right! That's a good one. Where am I? An infamous temp job. MJ Raynes, real estate this time. Wow. I'm hard to keep up with. The pay is $6.50 an hour; you sure can't beat that. OK, enough with the sarcasm. What's the scoop? So much for my big chance with Stanford. Fare thee well, 1985. Hello, who knows?

Went to Jamaica this summer with Sarah. We scraped up the money, saved every month and sold Jafra skin care products. And we had a great time. Then I went to Boston to visit Sher and Patrick, and now I just got back from DC. I tell you, what an exciting life. I don't have a whole hell of a lot to say. Why should I?

Sherry is getting ready to leave for London tomorrow. I'm sitting hoping that I get my phone call from Stanford. At this point, I don't believe the call will come, but tomorrow will tell.

Forget Knight. The way I feel, I can't even start seriously thinking about a man. It's funny to be back home. I've become friends with my neighbor Cole, but who cares how Cole could make me feel? No pursuit, fuck that. Hey, if it gravitates, it does; if not, oh well.

I'm really happy Sarah got her Payne Webber job. I hope it leads to big things.

Signing off and out for now.

P.S.: The past two weeks I've seen Cole. I'm still hot stuff with the men!

P.P.S.: Suicide still looks damn good. Definitely not off the horizon. I just need a foolproof method. Or however you spell that.

September 7, 1985 • The call didn't come. I don't think I can take it anymore. I feel so bad inside, and I can't go on like this. I don't know what to do except not be here. It just hurts too bad to try to stay focused and live each day. I tried all summer to go, go, go and do, do, do. I guess deep down inside I was hoping and praying it would make me feel better. Trying to act on what I have always believed, that if I just keep going forward, I can hang and I can deal with it.

But I can't deal with this. I want my baby. And I feel so flat. I told Mommy the truth. I've got so much pain inside that I can't even understand all of my own feelings. But it's there. I've been pushing myself, hoping that Stanford would be there for me, like a beacon or a life raft, something to hold on to. Now it's gone too, and I've got this overpowering feeling of nothingness, like with Knight when I wrote my poem "Inside and Out." That feeling feels like the only true emotion I have left.

September 9, 1985 • Hey, life, I'm sorry! Got to go, no more of this, no reason to stay anyway. Too bad I can't think of a closing poem maybe before who knows. Hey, I'm sorry I've got to go, it's not for anybody just myself that is how I know I've got to go, so badly just for me. I can't sit around being a martyr. I'm sorry. If not over-the-counter sleeping pills, there's got to be another way. I'll find it.

> *Staring toward a solid wall*
> *Trying to write a poem*
> *To find some meaning within*
> *Impossible*
> *Fuck it*
> *Fuck this*
> *No point*

Pointless
Why bother
Who gives a shit?
Not me anymore
Too tired of everything to care
Please be happy, I'm sorry I couldn't
I need oblivion not to feel.
All of a sudden the pain and the loss feels unbearable
Inside and Out
Now I am empty inside and out.
And I can't see beyond my yearning
And life feels empty.
And I'm thinking how I'd rather not be here.
I wait until Mommy leaves for work.
She stands in the doorway of my bedroom forever, as I lie in
my bed. She stands there as if by the sheer force of her will she
can hold me here and make the pain stop.
I have a plan.
I will turn on the oven until the gas is really flowing,
then I'll stick my head in and lay it down to rest.
Envision some peace. An end to this endless mind of mine,
tormenting me with its painful yet meaningless thoughts.
So I go to sleep crying and feeling that it's time to go.
But I've always been an all or nothing person. When I wake
up from a cry-induced sleep, 98% of me is ready to go.
But it's that 2% that hangs on that somehow won't let me do
it. Even as I lay there. 2% is 2% too much. I can't do it.
So I realize if I'm not going out.
And I can't go any further down.
I've got nowhere to go but up.

October 31, 1985 • We make tough choices. And anybody who thinks they are easy, or a cheap way out, needs to think again. Until you have walked a mile in someone else's shoes . . . I don't think there's much black and white in the situation. It can be very much a gray and mournful process. Life is not always made up of facile answers. And we each must do what is best in a given situation. Try to learn from it, share, and help others where we can. And keep going . . . I can see this now.

EPITAPH

Oblivion
Where you began
And where you had to end

But earth moves on
Though you are gone
As if you had never been

An ache in my throat
Tears in my eyes
Attest you are no more.

But I feel you
Within my heart
And can't quite go back to before.

I just want to tell you I'm sorry
And write something for you we can see
Though life will never have the chance to teach you
Life hurts, is what you taught me.

Could you lift this hurt I will ask
I know it's an unfair request
How can I ask this of you
When oblivion has been my bequest

I sit thinking
Why do I write this
For you
Or for my love and I
Perhaps it is done for us all
And the ties which we cannot deny

You are gone
But your memory does live on

Could you have saved the world?

Enough of pain, of love, regret
Be comforted
I won't forget.

Pack Tenacity

PACK TENACITY. SHEER GRIT. THE ABILITY TO hang in there. No matter what. There is a movie I really love, *The Last of the Mohicans* (the version with Daniel Day-Lewis). In it he yells across cascading water between him and his love as she is about to be taken captive, "No matter what you do, just stay alive. I will find you. Just stay alive," he's shouting. A request at its most primitive, most primal. It implies that it doesn't matter what you go through, where you go, how low . . . just stay here, on this planet, somehow, and "I will find you," he's telling her. They are, in fact, words we can each call out to ourselves. Even if you are lost. No matter what you go through, how dark it seems, how low or how hopeless. Somehow, find the will to survive. Just to stay here, even if it is holding on by a thread. Because if you hold on, just hold on . . . I found out, "you" **will** find you. And then, you can begin to build from there, having found yourself.

Survival and hope should be listed in the thesaurus as synonyms. I see that now.

SLAVE DANCE

Hear the whisper of the sound
the rhythm of the beat
I can feel it in my soul
though dancing with bound feet
to execute a pirouette I simply tilt my head
for arms that chain behind one's back
cannot be used instead
my grace is not within my leap
or twirls up off the floor
it shines from deep within my glance
and how my spirit soars

7

The Force Behind
My Rainbow

RAINBOW
So you're looking for a spinning top
Where you can pull the string
You will make a motion
And bright colors I will bring
You will watch me twirl around
While I have no control
And it is only when you stop
That I will cease to roll
But no I say this is not so
For I must fight to be
The force behind my rainbow
And my destiny.

November 5, 1985 • The E train was packed as usual, as it raced away from the Fifty-ninth Street platform. I fought to keep my small space and hold on tight to the bar stretched over my head, thankful that the person in front of me appeared to be preparing to exit at the next stop, Fifth Avenue, where the train load always starts to thin out some. I had already taken a nap for the first half hour of the train ride. I've become an expert at standing up and sleeping at the same time. I reserve the section of time before we get to Twenty-third Street, my stop, to think about and prepare for the day. I was smiling thinking about how life is.

Next month I am scheduled to go visit Sherry in London! Right now I work at Manning, Selvage & Lee, a huge public relations firm, where I am a coordinator for one of the top company executives, Jan Fenner.

I have settled into life here in New York, and have done a lot of building back up in the past few months. I've gotten a job, earned some money, sent in my Stanford Law School application and applied to three other law schools in California. I am having a good time living with Mommy, enjoying being in the same city as Andrea, hanging out with friends, and having fun just being buddies with new men in my life.

Life is good. It's taken me several months to see that, but here I am. Time has passed, water under the bridge, and all that. I came very close to the end in September. I guess only a few people will ever understand how close. But I know, and I'll remember. Has it made me stronger? I don't know, but I believe so.

I still think about Knight, but the edge is gone off the pain, and I know that I have things to live for. I guess I've been working through my despair and am again inspired with my love of life, all the more cherished since I came close to giving it up.

The more I learn about this society and life experiences, the more I want to be able to truly work to tip the scales of justice and help people. I believe that law school will be an entree into my being able to work to contribute, whether it is in improving the state of educational opportunities, housing laws, or the rights of people under the law.

I believe there is a need for folks my age to roll up our sleeves and get busy.

I redid the entire application process for Stanford, including a new essay on why I want to go to law school. It gave me the opportunity to again look into my heart as to my reasons for wanting to attend law school. After considering everything I had gone through to get to this point, the fact that I still wanted to push myself and try again confirmed how strong my commitment is to doing this.

This time around, I am increasingly clear that California is where I am supposed to go. Stanford is it for me! I have faith that I am going to get straight in, no wait list, no rejection.

Meanwhile, I am living life here, not trying to burn the candle at both ends but more to live life simply, fully, and joyfully, to continue to get my head together. Even on the tough days, this feels good.

November 6, 1985 • Manning, Selvage & Lee is very much a corporate public relations environment. We have clients like Procter & Gamble, Godiva Chocolates, and other huge names. I anticipate this is a place where I can learn much. Looking back on my job at *City Streets*, I realize that George Masters and the instant responsibility he gave me, treating me like a producer rather than an intern, was a phenomenon that won't always occur. Witness the Insurance Institute for Highway Safety. Still, my hopes are high that I will get to do a variety of work. I never mind the grunt work. I am quite good at all of it, trained well on my many temp jobs. But I love writing and creatively approaching projects, and I hope I get to do that kind of work here, too.

So far, I like my desk and my nameplate. I like some of the work I do. I have to do a lot of extra work for my boss, Jan, like organizing a party at her house tomorrow night. Still, I have fun with work like that—the caterer, the flowers—I love organizing. And I love parties.

November 7, 1985 • I walked over to Jan's house on Twenty-fifth Street to make sure everything was completed; the food that was set up and out so far looked lovely. I was not invited; she would take it from here, she and the servers, bartender, and so on. But that's OK. I was glad to be relieved at the end of the day. A job well done.

I raced to the F train to go meet Andrea at the Old Stand on Fifty-seventh and celebrate. Then we booked over to Forty-second Street after that to do some last-minute shoe shopping. Then I headed back to Queens, a train and bus ride away.

This breaking into the world of work and getting past entry level responsibilities can be quite challenging, I realize. When I first graduated from college, I had visions of immediately jumping into an intense and satisfying job. Not that I mind paying my dues. I guess I just wasn't aware of what that meant. And since I am not willing to move to Podunk, USA, to become a weatherwoman there, I've got to hang on for the ride. Looking forward to law school!

A guy on the train got on yelling at the top of his lungs about the cost of tea in China. Folks sure are wild on the train, I thought, engrossed in my Harlequin, but hey, I'm used to it.

December 1, 1985 • I've been having a great time catching up with old friends since moving back to New York. Justine and I have drifted apart over the years. I used to try to call her some, but she seldom called back. I hear she graduated, and she and her little girl moved to Maryland. Sometimes our not being in touch makes me sad. Mostly though, I think about all the great times that we shared, and it's OK that our lives have gone in different directions.

I miss Sarah and DC, but I go down to visit a lot and spend many a weekend, so it kind of feels like the best of all worlds. I've been hanging out a lot with my old homeroom friend, Priscilla, the girl who signaled me not to open my mouth when Enid was going off on me. She stayed in New York and went to college in the city, to Fordham University (where my mom and grandmother attended). Now she's out too, working at a marketing job in Queens. It doesn't sound like much fun, the way she tells it, but we make up for it by doing all sorts of fun and exciting things on the weekends like dancing, walking around the city, and catching free exhibits. She lives about fifteen minutes from Rochdale, so in high school sometimes Priscilla, Sherry, and I would go to the movies together on Saturday.

Now this year the three of us will have the opportunity to hang out once again, since Priscilla and I are both going to visit Sherry in London! We can't wait. I was smart, because when I got my job at MS&L, I negotiated my time for the trip to London, which I had already planned. So other than continuing to save up our money, we are all set.

Priscilla's family is from the Dominican Republic. When I go over to visit, I practice my Spanish with her mom and learn some Dominican recipes to add to my culinary repertoire. Priscilla doesn't like spending time at her house. A few of her older brothers are kind of mean, and she doesn't feel there's anything she can do about it. So on the weekends when we hang out, sometimes she spends the weekend at our house. Mommy is really cool about this and always welcomes my friends who need a place to stay. The three of us hang out together, go out to eat and stay up late into the night, drinking tea and talking about life.

Things at work aren't going great, but to tell the truth I'm really not worried about it. I am going to law school in the fall, and meanwhile I will do my best at any job I take on, just as I always do, but I am not going to trip about it. I've learned a lot about balancing my emotions more lately. I guess I am finally learning to chalk some things up to experience, a skill I wondered if I'd ever have, back in Jamaica High School.

At the end of my first day of work, Jan, my boss, patted me on the head, like I was our dog, Pepper, and said, "Good work." Folks on the job kind of look at me askance when they hear who I am the "lucky" coordinator for. The word is she is very exacting and very cruel, as if you have to be that in order to run the department. I don't think so. I don't let the rumors scare me. I do my job, and I do it well. She was very happy with the party arrangements. We'll see what happens on down the road.

In other breaking news: I've been having a blast with Cole. He lives in my building in Rochdale. After all this time living in the same building, we have discovered each other. Since the time I bumped into him on the bus, shortly after moving back to Queens, we have been talking and found we really enjoyed each other's conversation. It doesn't hurt that he is fine. Fine, finer even than Andrew from DC fine. Or maybe it's also that I like him better. Cole has the most dazzling smile. With Cole, I can be myself, relax, and have crazy fun. It's not a tense or uptight interaction, as it often was with Knight and it's not all serious, as it grew to be with Chris. To tell the truth, I believe it is just what the doctor ordered. I think I brighten Cole's life, too. At least, that's how it feels!

December 2, 1985 • I can't believe it.

Priscilla was robbed.

OK, well, it wasn't that simple. Here's what happened.

She called me at my job this afternoon to tell me that she had some exciting news, that she'd just had this amazing experience, and that she was going to come into some money. "Our trip to visit Sher will be even better, and I can give you some money to help you with law school," she told me excitedly.

What happened? I asked.

"I was coming back from lunch when I found this wallet on the ground," Priscilla bubbled into the phone. "Well, actually, I and this other woman found it at the same time. And in it there were these bonds, worth a lot of money, but we had no way for anyone to claim them because there was no ID, and then this woman said . . ."

As I listened to the story, I got this sinking feeling inside. I remembered the time years and years ago that my mother told the story of two people who tried to con her out of her money when all three of them happened to be walking by a "lost" wallet on the ground. Priscilla's story sounded suspiciously familiar.

I focused again on her story, as she continued her breathless tale.

"So then, I gave them some money," she said.

That did it.

You what? I asked. Where are they now? I went on urgently.

"Oh, they're at the Learner's store, where one of them works," Priscilla said. Quick, I said, get down to Learner's and find them. Get your money back, I shouted.

Priscilla banged the receiver down.

I sat hoping that what I was now thinking wasn't true, that somehow, I'd misunderstood the story.

My desk phone rang. Manning, Sel—I was interrupted by the sound of sobs. It was Priscilla. "They're gone," she cried. "They're gone, and they've taken my money."

Priscilla, sweetie, I'm here, I said as I tried to send loving vibes over the wire. All I could do was listen as she sobbed out her story.

What had happened was that once they all "found" the wallet, the two women suggested that they split the bonds in the wallet, since there was no name on the wallet or means of returning it. They agreed that each should put up collateral to trust the others. Priscilla's collateral was first. That's where Priscilla's money came in.

Priscilla and I spent the weekend hanging out. She went to the police station to try to identify the thieves. We know them only by the names she's made up for them: Little Bit and Toughie. Eventually, we applied our sense of humor to the situation, and spent many hours reenacting the crime, entertaining friends with just how crazy it was. Especially the part where Toughie is driving down 168th Street, saw a cop car down the street, and did a hard left, saying, "Oh, we can't go down that street." Clue? But the police say once you are in the throes of the pocketbook-drop scam, you can't see the forest for the trees. Or the con that's staring you in the face. We can now laughingly agree.

Priscilla never got her money back. But maybe the lesson was infinitely more valuable (for all of us). She worked hard to save money so she could still go to London.

December 12, 1985 • London trip! It's incredible being back after all these years. Priscilla and I have packed a ton of stuff. Way too much. But that's OK.

Sherry met us at the airport, adorable in her new poodle haircut. Priscilla and I have our hair in our expert braid hairstyles. We are sooo good; we have even started a braid business. We don't charge enough, though, and our hands are raw when we're done. Still, we love doing it.

December 22, 1985 • By the time we got to London we were so sleepy from all of our hanging out back in NY that we never did truly adjust to the time zone. That meant we slept really late into each morning. Then we would get out and race all through London to make up for the time lost. We did the Tower of

London in only sixteen minutes, including all of ten seconds spent admiring the crown jewels.

We took fashion shots (of ourselves) throughout London, and we went dancing to funky London clubs and hung out with Sherry's new friends, the stars of the play *Little Shop of Horrors*. Sherry told the story of how once, when she was hobnobbing with all the funky London crowd, George Michael pinched her on the butt.

We went out to the beautiful English countryside, soaking up sights and sounds of this country town that spans centuries. My love of history and ancient and bygone times was renewed in the streets of London. Cathedrals, like St. Paul's, statues, and other sights made me again realize what a young country America truly is. I thought, too, about the fact that while the United States is so young, the land itself has been there for centuries, inhabited by Native Americans long before the Pilgrims and explorers touched its soil.

To make ends meet in addition to classes and her internship, Sherry has used to good effect her bartender's training that she took for fun in Boston last year. She works in an English pub, for a bloke named Micky. She sees another side of London through her work there. Money is still tight for all of us, but we never let that stop us from making whatever we are trying to make happen . . . happen. Still, by the end of the trip, we were scraping up money and down to nothing. Good thing we had our plane tickets, and Sherry managed to hook up a ride for us all to the airport.

Sherry will be home in a few weeks. She's got finals to get through first.

January 6, 1986 • I did some great writing for public relations campaigns for Jan.

Unfortunately, I also made my first big mistake today. I was horrified. And boy, was it big. My mistake was in arranging a client meeting for her that turned out to be in Chicago, while I thought it was in New York. Talk about pissed, Jan was furious. Not that I blame her. Nothing I could say made the least bit of difference, especially not my profuse apologies. So I just shut up and made the flight arrangements. She made it to JFK to fly to Chicago with only a few minutes to spare.

Thank God it's Friday. I can't wait to get home.

January 8, 1985 • Hanging out with Cole gives me a different perspective on life at Rochdale. Cole likes to tease me about how Sherry and I didn't come out and play around our way when we were kids. He makes jokes about "our little faces plastered to the window." No they weren't, I say laughing. We weren't even home. "Yeah sure," Cole grins. We lived in the same building all these years, but we never really got to know each other. It's fun doing it now.

I love watching Cole play football, tight end, all six foot four of him. I don't know much about the game, even though I was a Rifflette. Still, I love watching his games. I like going to his house and hanging out, talking and feeling good. He even teases me and says that I shouldn't wax my lip because he likes the faint brush of hair there; he thinks it's sexy. "I'll never kiss those lips again," he jokes. We laugh.

Laughter feels good.

I feel mine truly coming back.

WELCOME BACK
my spirit sings
a cry long overdue
Welcome back
I long to say
Yes, I have missed you, too.
Welcome back

It's been too long
Since last I saw you smile
Felt your presence, heard your voice
now please would you stay a while?

February 12, 1986 • In addition to work, I have become a part of a campaign to elect a district assemblyman right at home here in Queens. My primary responsibility is to analyze the current state of our community, take the pulse of the community, talk with folks to learn what their main concerns and needs are right now, and then design ways to propose improvements. Also, I am to evaluate current strategies for change and to work with the campaign manager on concepts for implementation and, of course, for speeches. The process is an exciting although sometimes frustrating one.

Usually I take my honorary little sister, Vivian, with me. Even though she is only fifteen, she is really intelligent and insightful. When I drive us home at night after a meeting, I enjoy hashing out with Vivian what makes sense and what doesn't. We generate further ideas and suggestions for the campaign, many of which we take to the next meeting and place on the table.

Vivian's mother passed away a few years ago. The whole family are dear family friends of ours. Vivian's older sister is away at college. I am an honorary older sister to Vivian, and a friend. These days, she spends a lot of time at our house with Mommy and me. I know the feeling of having a household transition almost overnight. I don't know the feeling of losing your mother, but I know this particular road is painful and challenging for her. I do my best to be there with her. We inhabit a sensitive world together where we meet and connect. We talk and hang out together, and she confides in me. Actually, I confide in her as well; she is a very insightful young lady.

She teases me that I am old, at twenty-two. I tell her, One day you'll be twenty-two, and some fifteen-year-old will be telling you how "old" you are. My theory is, we all get to be one age for one year, no more, no less. Thing is to appreciate and enjoy it. We laugh. And then she gets the last word with, "But then, you'll be twenty-nine, almost thirty." Wow, I say, that feels a hell of a long way away.

April 30, 1986 • Tonight after work I met Daddy for dinner in Midtown. Since I've been back home we occasionally get together after work. He updates me about the latest happenings at work—with his settlement house and how he continues to work diligently to serve the community—and I share with him what's going on with me.

We don't talk about the past. Just the present and the future. Sometimes I wish that we could talk about the past, but I don't know that any conversation could ever help me to make sense of it. So I figure it's a bust trying to understand any of the many "whys" in my head and in my Daddy's Girl poem. (Which I've never shown Daddy.) I guess I have to accept that they'll go unanswered. C'est la vie.

I shared with Daddy about applying again to Stanford. "I hope it happens for you, Sharon," Daddy said.

March 2, 1986 • The guy Priscilla is seeing is Phillip. Phil is studying to be an undertaker. He dresses kind of conservatively and wears black a lot.

Cilla and I devised a master plan to pull the best joke on Cole and Phil! It took a bit of work and planning to come together, but Saturday night we put the plan into action.

We had Cole and Phillip over for dinner. We cooked this really terrible meal. Set the table breathtakingly lovely. And we wore beautiful clothes. I wore my red suede dress and Priscilla looked gorgeous in black. We spent quite a while getting our hair just perfect. About fifteen minutes after they were due to arrive, Phil rang the bell.

An hour later we were still waiting for Cole. He is always late. He always has "stops to make." Why do some guys always have stops to make? We wonder. What's up with that? I'm not used to this way of doing things. The guys I have dated in the past showed up when they said they were going to. Cole is a breed unto himself, with disturbing similarities to a lot of other homies.

Finally, an hour and a half late, Cole showed up, his usual charming self. Phil was kind of pissed that Cole was so late. He's a big man, too, and he was hungry. Don't worry gentlemen, I said in my best Susie Homemaker tone, we have a delicious meal in store for you. I flashed a smile Cole's way. His face showed he was thinking that his charm works every time.

"Dinner is served," we said, ringing a little bell that Mommy keeps in the windowsill. Candlelight on the table reflected the crystal goblets we would serve the iced tea in, since none of us drink much, and Cole is in training. We even made them hold hands and say grace. We could barely hold our laughs back as we hovered around their chairs to serve them, really overdoing it. We were acting like those girls who will bend over backwards for a man to keep his attention.

"Oh, let me get your napkin for you," Priscilla lovingly told Phillip. I hope you'll enjoy this dinner, I said to Cole as I set a plate before him. We worked ever so hard to make this special meal for you both.

Starving, Cole sawed at the tough steak. At $2.69 for the pack of steak, it was not a particularly good cut, especially after we'd cooked it for more than two hours. It took him a while to succeed in sawing off a piece. Meanwhile, Phil had chosen the corn to sink his teeth into. He had a problem however, since it was frozen corn on the cob and we had boiled it for a mere two minutes; it was still solid as the proverbial rock.

Cilla, I said, the rice turned out divinely. "Yes, Sharon," Priscilla replied, sliding me a smile, laughter barely restrained beneath her words. "The rolls are a bit hard," she continued (we had saved them from dinner at a restaurant the previous weekend), "but our recipe for the steak is perfect."

The poor guys were giving it such a valiant effort, we couldn't take it anymore. Besides, we didn't want them to get full on this stuff; we wanted them to enjoy the real meal we had cooked in their honor.

"This isn't the real dinner!" We cracked up. "Got ya!" We shouted.

"Thank God," Phil said.

Cole however, didn't want to give up his plate until he saw the other option. Trust me, I reassured him, it's good. We're really good cooks.

"Yeah, right," Cole said. I had to wrestle him for his plate. He finally let me win.

Later, after a delicious meal of sautéed chicken and shrimp, we relaxed leisurely in the living room. They promised to get us back. I was ever so slightly nervous when I saw the dangerous glint in Cole's eye. "Not possible," Cilla and I said. "We're too good."

March 1, 1986 • I am no longer at MS&L. I became the fourth in a long line of coordinators that Jan decided she was better off without. I wasn't too downtrodden, since frankly I was feeling the same way.

The human resources director thought I was a valuable asset to the company, just not to Jan, so she offered to place me in a new department. No, I decided, I think I'd rather just make a clean

break of it. Although I find public relations wc
this is in fact a pretty corporate environment. It c
creativity that I felt at the television station. The wu... .. ...
nications is a vastly varied and complex one, I am learning. Glad
for the experience, I am also glad to move on. I took my cool
nameplate, a modern black design with white letters. Who else can
use the nameplate "Sharon Simpson"?

I called my good old temp agency once again.

March 3, 1986 • Monday morning, found me at a new, two-
day gig on Fifty-seventh and Sixth answering phones. Over the
years, my receptionist skills have become outstanding. I don't
mind being a receptionist. In my heart I know that this time
is a blessing, not having to push myself right now, in the ways
that will challenge me next year in law school. I am determined
that when I get to law school, I will pull out all the stops to
bust it out. So this time right now, with low pressure, is time
well spent. I am thankful I can see that and that I am not
excessively driven to have to have "the job," like some of my
classmates. There's time enough for that, I know. Besides, to
tell the truth, I enjoy being a receptionist. I like talking to lots
of people and helping them have a better day because they have
received great service.

I am closer to Andrea's job. And it's a hop, skip, and a jump to
the Old Stand from here.

March 7, 1986 • GCI temp agency hooked me up with the perfect long-term temp job. Part-time working at Citibank. I like it.
I am really good at word processing and everything else involved
in this job. It suits me. I go there and put the same energy into it
as I did into my job at MS&L or WCVB-TV. Respect for myself,
those I work with, and the opportunity is what I believe in.

Meanwhile, I live life, have fun, and prepare for SLS in the fall, continuing to have faith that I am going to be admitted. Even though it's only been a few days, the people at Citibank said, "Oh, you're really smart," as though they are surprised. Thank you, I responded. Some of them think I am "dumb," however, for being there. I don't let their attitude bother me any. I feel good.

There's this one guy, Mr. Clarke, "Nate," who is so funny. He thinks that because he is a young black vice president, I am going to get all excited over his "overtures." I don't care what kind of work you do; it is the person you are that matters to me. He's a trip, showing me his office and trying to touch me. He thinks I am a "skeezer." That's funny. Some guys really crack me up. I just laugh and think how silly he is.

March 8, 1986 • A truly phenomenal friendship I have formed is with Andrea's cousin Lance. We hang out and spend a lot of time together, building an incredible friendship. I have fabulous conversations on the phone with Lance. He is one of the most awesome people I've ever met. He is determined, powerful, and dedicated in how he addresses life, his work, his family, and his friendships. He is confident, and it shows in how he carries himself. Not only do I like him, I admire him. It's a good feeling.

We support each other, making it, growing, progressing, dealing with whatever the day has to offer, and sharing our lessons with each other. Most of the time, I think we do a great job of it.

The more I think about it, the gladder I am that I have had this year to get my head together. This is a blessing.

March 10, 1986 • Andrea, Priscilla and I prepared a celibacy party for me to celebrate a year of no sex. We have a special tea toast. My anniversary feels good. I know where my head is at, and I feel good in who I am, what I stand for, the lessons I am learning, and where I want to go.

March 12, 1986 • For Mommy and me, it is now our turn to live alone together; Sherry is completing her senior year at BU. Again I am conscious of what a blessing it is that I have had this extra year. Sometimes things that we think don't work out actually are working for the best, if we can hang in there long enough to see it. While we certainly have our financial challenges, we share a world of fun and joy together.

We spend time reminiscing. In the midst of memory, this one came to me. It brought a smile to both our faces.

XMAS LIGHTS AND MEMORIES
I remember when we were kids
At Christmas time
And Mommy putting up the Christmas lights
in different designs each year
On the terrace of our apartment
Sherry and I standing in the doorway of the terrace,
Our robes flapping in the freezing New York cold
Watching Mommy string the lights
How could she weave such magic in the cold, we never thought
That's what Mommies are for.

Mommy's new job is going really well as an academic supervisor throughout the five boroughs of New York City, with an innovative program called CSIP that she was selected to participate in by the Queens superintendent of schools. I am so proud of her.

March 14, 1986 • I keep checking the mail to see if my letter has come from Stanford yet.

March 15, 1986 • My letter came.

Fantastic news, I'm going to Stanford!

After all the agonizing and the pain and the perseverance, I have been admitted. Mommy and I went out to celebrate.

March 20, 1986 • I gotta admit, I'd like to spend more time hanging out with Cole, but he is so elusive. I think he likes it that way. Sometimes I don't even know if he likes me. OK, that's an extreme exaggeration; I know he likes me. But I guess that doesn't mean you live happily ever after. Obviously. These days, though, that's cool. I don't make up as many fairy stories.

I don't know. I'm just trying to reap joy from each day. That's my new big thing, reaping joy. I'm not always doing it so well, but I intend to try.

March 22, 1986 • We party in the city most weekends—I, Andrea, Priscilla, Lincoln, who is back in NY since graduation from BU, my old buddies Joyce and Toni, and Lance, and a bunch of his friends. I am so happy that all of our friendships have merged so gradually and so well, in essence the continued building of community. Our favorite place to go dancing is at the Garage. It doesn't even open till midnight. So these days, we have cranked partying up to a whole new level, and with a huge crew. I'm loving it.

Last weekend when Sherry was home, Sherry, Priscilla and I were driving into the city to meet the gang. As we were walking to the elevator from our apartment, Mommy, unusually, followed us to the elevator. The whole time, she kept describing what to do if the car were to hydroplane. She was really worried about the bad rainstorm. Yes, I hear you Mommy, I said, not really listening. Still she kept talking.

Sure enough, on the FDR Drive, a car in front of us stopped suddenly. I had no choice but to brake. The car began spinning and hydroplaned. The words of my mother came back to me. I did what I would never have thought to do otherwise, I turned into the spin.

Thank goodness we were OK. I've always tried to listen to Mommy's insights, but after this experience, if she tells me something she senses, I am going to make sure I am totally tuned in.

April 24, 1986 • Today I will allow myself the luxury of feeling good about my future. Feel good; that will be my new motto for 1986. No matter what. No matter how hard it gets. Feel good. Whether I am concerned about financial aid or my outfit looking lousy or whatever.

Keep on feeling great.

Starting now! Yeah!

May 4, 1986 • Mommy and I are doing a lot of shopping and planning for law school. It is serious get-in-gear time to be ready for September. Sometimes I stop and marvel once again at how great it feels to feel good. And how thankful I am to be here.

I went to the Stanford Law School acceptance dinner, this time as an entering member of the class of 1989. In fact, I became an informal recruiter along with the dean. I was so enthusiastic and sure that it was the right place for me, I found myself strongly encouraging others.

May 28, 1986 • Still sometimes I have my melancholy moments. But I know them for what they are. Melancholy moments.

I USED TO LOVE YOU.
Whether foolish, wonderful, or unavoidable
It's true
I used to love you

Whether displaced, mistaken, or unappreciated
It's true
I used to love you
Whether buried, fallen from grace, or forgotten
It's true I used to love you
I still do.

July 15, 1986 • Sarah's ex-boyfriend's birthday, I still recall. We heard that he got married last year.

Here I sit in a Lexington Avenue shoe store because some stupid MF stepped on and broke the strap to my shoe while trying to give me a very tired rap. What a laugh, except it's not funny. Oh, well.

August 16, 1986 • Sherry graduated from BU! She will be remaining in Boston with Patrick and working there. Again, we are city hopping. I am leaving New York to go to California, Sherry will be in Massachusetts, and Mommy will be in New York. That part will be hard, but we are all pursuing our dreams and our lives, and we support each other long distance. We have learned how to do that well.

Lance and I have vowed to continue our friendship, wherever we are, and I know we will.

Vivian and I have promised to write to each other. I am hopeful that the year we have been able to spend together has made a positive difference for her. I am going to miss my girl. We vow to talk frequently, as well.

I have been thinking lately, when I can actually grab a moment to profoundly think, about my relationship journey thus far and truly making peace with it. Thinking back to those long-ago days when I agonized over not having had a boyfriend and knowing now that there is nothing to be ashamed of. Part of what I realize is that the journey is what it is, and we can't know what is going to happen or with whom. In that spirit, I approach the future and say good-bye to the past.

I don't understand Knight, I mean, the emotional side of the man. What makes him tick. I don't understand his feelings for me, then or now. I don't know what we were meant to be in this life or what we will be. It's in the hands of fate.

Knight came to say good-bye to me and to wish me luck before I left for Stanford. I don't know why. I don't think he does, either. Oh, well, I can't be bothered to worry about that now, although I will write him and hope that he writes in return.

Cole says we missed our time and that when I go away to law school, I will forget about him. He'd be a tough person to forget. Or perhaps he is right. But I know he is an enigma and a good guy as well.

I am shipping most of my things out to California, including the television I worked so hard to buy junior year. I hope it gets there in one piece. I am also taking several suitcases with me when I fly out to San Francisco airport, trusting that I am taking all I need. At long last. California, here I come.

Pack Healing

PACK HEALING. LOVING TIMES SOOTHE OUR wounded spirit, mind, and body and give us the chance to heal and grow. I pack Healing and the loving balm that comes from allowing myself the time to feel and be with my emotions and, ultimately, to heal.

When we take time for Healing, there is a trust that everything is going to be all right. That we can afford to allow ourselves the time to heal and know that it is time we'll be blessed to have, to come through on the other side. Sometimes it is important not to worry about tomorrow but to heal today and to trust that tomorrow is there for us. Don't rush the Healing; ride it like a gentle wave that rolls into one's spirit.

Restore, reconcile, settle, accept, embrace.

8

Lyrics of Survival

September 7, 1986 • He snuck up behind me.

I stood talking with Lisa, another new student, our feet curling in the cold sand. We were imagining what our first day of school would be like. It was weird meeting all these classmates at a beach to embark upon one of the most challenging, serious journeys of our lives. Law school.

I was trying so hard to be serious and weighty and earnest as we hazarded guesses about our classes.

Then he pushed me. Grabbed me. Dragged me. Straight into the water.

The Pacific Ocean danced ice cold along my back. I fell as waves leaped over me, drenching my light summer outfit. Blasts of water shot me to my knees. Hands outstretched, I gripped air.

Elusive as the dignity I possessed moments before. Now adrift at sea.

That guy pushed me, I thought in disbelief, as I managed to stand up against the onslaught of the waves.

I struggled toward shore.

His laughter welcomed me back onto the chilly sand. Unrelenting mountains surrounded us. A suddenly unfriendly beach.

I can't believe you did that, I challenged. What's your problem?

"It was funny. You wanted to go in, didn't you? I heard you saying earlier how you wished it were warm enough for you to go in. I just helped you out."

As I listened to his silly explanations, the beginnings of a poem started forming in my mind. I just helped you out. In search of your desire. Not the water's welcome. Just the underlying fire . . . No, that wasn't the point. The point was, I was wet. And this guy pushed me in. Still, I could see that arguing with him was futile, especially in my wet clothes that left little to the imagination. I backed away from him, realizing my presence only enhanced his joy.

Just stay away from me, I said deliberately.

"Are you all right?" Lisa asked me.

Yeah, I guess, I said, just wet and embarrassed.

I was surprised I was able to acknowledge that to her, especially since I just met her. This all felt so new I didn't know what to make of anything, not after that wack experience. Somehow though, she was easy to talk to.

I looked around. It didn't seem that anybody had noticed, or cared, for that matter. Except Lisa. She'd tried to help me, but being what looked to be only a bit above five feet, she'd been no match for the six feet of Levy, our wacky classmate. And . . . my hair got wet, and I didn't have a mirror. I guess this guy didn't know any better. Or care.

I may be wet, but I am not going to let this ruin my day, I thought. We went on talking and having fun. It just so happened that Lisa had an extra pair of shorts with her. And this attractive guy in our class, Matthew, whom I'd talked with earlier on the beach, lent me the shirt off his back. I like the way that part worked out. So I moved on past the silliness and continued to enjoy the unexpected as well as the expected in the day.

This is my fourth day in California. Neither the beach, which I shockingly discovered didn't have a boardwalk where hungry people can eat (like back home in New York), nor school itself, were as I'd anticipated. Then again, it had been difficult to imagine.

I always knew I was supposed to come to California. It was just a question of how and when. Now those questions are answered, and what remains to be seen is what happens next.

I traveled a long journey to get here to Stanford Law School. If the first four days are anything to go by, I know I am in for a rocky ride. Good thing "hanging on" and persevering are my specialties. I figure I am going to need all my skills, academic and survival, and then some . . .

The best thing about this tilt-a-whirl day was that I met Lisa.

September 10, 1986 • Lisa is a first-year too, which is how we ended up on the same field trip. She didn't bring any food, either. She's from Massachusetts, near Boston.

I like Lisa. She is extremely down to earth (definitely not the case with many folks here) and has this way of looking you straight in the eye and never wavering. That's actually a good description of her personality. She's twenty-four, has startling blue-green eyes and short, curly, black hair that is almost as frizzy as mine.

Our first-year class is an extremely diverse lot. We are called 1Ls. There are students in our graduating class of 1989 from all parts of the country as well as from many countries throughout the world. There are people of all ages and experience levels: classmates with families, classmates on their fourth and fifth degrees, and classmates on their second and even third career—journalists, medical doctors, scientists, investment bankers, Olympic runners, you name it, they are here. It's pretty amazing.

In the midst of trying to make sense of law school, thick casebooks, and deceptively sunny Palo Alto, Lisa and I found ourselves in the same small section. That means we have all our classes together: criminal law, civil procedure, contracts, and the mysterious torts.

In torts, Lisa sits across from me. The room is shaped like a horseshoe. Professor Ellickson stands in the middle or strides around the floor, almost like an actor on stage, very high energy.

It is actually a pretty exciting class. People really get into it, and the discussion today was very lively. Professor Ellickson (a transfer from Yale Law School) is a rigorous teacher. When he says "Ms. Simpson," it is all I ever imagined about law school and more. Today, I finally found out what a tort actually is. Roughly, a tort is a wrongful act where an injury has occurred, for which you can sue.

September 12, 1986 • After class, Lisa and I walked back to our new homes.

"Where do you live, Sharon?" Lisa asked. "I live in the law school dorm."

Oh, I said, don't think I'm crazy, but I live in Manzanita.

"The trailer park?"

It's not that I was crazy electing to live there, I explained, but from my read of the Stanford brochures it was the only place on campus that you were guaranteed to get your own room. Also, the adventurous side of me, which gets free reign most of the time, admits to having had fantasies of living in a trailer since my Barbie's Country Camper days.

"I know what you mean," Lisa said, laughing. "It's the adventurous side of me that usually guides me in life as well."

We smiled at each other.

At the trailer park I've got two roommates. Catherine, who just returned from a year of study and work in Australia, blond, blue-eyed and originally from Berkeley, California is also a 1L;

we have already become good friends. And Inga from Iceland, quiet and taciturn, is in a social science master's program. I think Inga misses her boyfriend.

The trailer is kind of flimsy. Last week, Inga's foot went through the floor.

October 8, 1986 • Lisa is getting very involved in the East Palo Alto Community Law Project. That is a legal clinic established by Stanford Law Students a few years ago to provide legal assistance to the under-serviced population on the other side of wealthy Palo Alto. She has done this kind of work before, back in Massachusetts. I admire her dedication.

I, too, am getting involved in programs here at school. I've started reporting for the law school newspaper, the *Stanford Law Journal*. I have also become very involved with the Black Law Students Association (BLSA). I am now the co-chair of BLSA's Political Social Change Committee. It looks as though, from what I can see so far, we have a lot of "material" to work with. There are only fourteen of us black students out of a class of 175. That makes us, in fact, one of the largest black classes Stanford Law School has ever had. There are no black professors on staff here at the law school. There are rumors about a black professor who was here briefly last year from Harvard. He taught Constitutional Law. I am curious to learn the story of what happened. People seem uncomfortable talking about it. Painful subject?

October 24, 1986 • The second month of law school is coming to an end. Comparing it to the time I stood up in front of all those people and did my *Colored Girls* monologue with strep throat is not working as an analogy anymore. This feels harder. Not in the obvious way of tough classes. Classes are not easy; far from it, but the challenge is more difficult to describe.

This fall, as first-years, I'm sure we have all promised ourselves many things. I promised myself I'd work hard and not play much, that for once I'll focus upon my schoolwork to the exclusion of all else, including friends and relationships. I don't know what Lisa promised herself, although, knowing Lisa, she is probably keeping her word.

Me, I've broken mine . . . and we have become friends.

Friendship in law school is a funny thing, especially first year. First year is one of those times when no matter where you are from, what your past achievements are, how many degrees, accolades and "firsts" you've earned, you are all in the same boat. It's kind of like in that old movie *The Paper Chase*, when they say, "Look to the left of you and look to the right of you; one of you won't be here . . ." (or words to that effect). Even though at Stanford they didn't say that, it's pretty darn intense. Folks who have been confident of their abilities all of their lives are suddenly feeling just a bit unnerved, or in some cases, really scared. Me, I don't think I am your typical law student, whatever that means. I've never been one to solely measure myself by my academic prowess. You have to fight not to get caught up in this scene. Still, this place is a scary transition, to what I'm not sure yet. But I find myself working hard to hold onto Me.

Because everything is so intense (with people struggling for their place, or to "get it," as in to understand what is going on, or to finish the volumes and volumes of unfamiliar reading, and so on), many people seem to have no time to spend seriously relating to each other.

Taking the time to develop a strong emotional friendship and, when your friend needs you, not putting work first, seems out of the ordinary here. I don't know what I would do without my dear friends or the activities in which we've become involved. They keep me going.

Also, on the score of class itself, I've noticed that even though Lisa and I are both quite expressive people, talking in law school class feels like a whole other animal, so to speak. It feels like the perspective with which we sometimes view a case, when we are talking about it together before class, is vastly different from the perspective from which class discussions analyze it. This environment takes some serious getting used to. I am sorting through what I feel about this experience thus far. What I know is, I am glad I came. What I don't know is, why do I feel so different?

I realized though, today, that it has been quite a while since I wrote a poem. Considering how poetry is such a huge part of who I am, this thought caught me by surprise. But I think here, being inundated with the process of beginning to "think like a lawyer," the poetic side of me is suffering. I refuse to let that happen, whatever the cost.

POETRY OF MIND
Living in my head
Dancing from my eyes
Seeing past the lies
Breathing through my life
Spirit of my soul
Song of my heart
Poetry of mind

November 29, 1986 • "How was your camping trip with Matthew and little Morrow?" Lisa asked me as we hung out eating lunch. She with a grilled cheese and coffee, I with grilled cheese and tea.

It was great. You know, I guess the thing that strikes me about this relationship is how right we both felt, so quickly, I told her. There were and still are no cat-and-mouse games. I'm sure that part of the acceleration of our relationship is being in school, but still, it's amazing to me how quickly he and I have grown inseparable ever since we met on that beach field trip.

Lisa smiled, recalling.

You remember, I told you how I actually met his son, Morrow, first? I continued. There I was playing with this adorable three-year-old, coaxing him out of his shyness, when all of a sudden I looked up and Matthew was there looking at me, his head cocked to one side and his eyes smiling into mine.

"Yes, Sharon, but did you know then, at that moment, that this was really special?"

You know, Lisa, I always say that when we really fell in love was in San Francisco on our first "date." That always makes me very happy because I think that's pretty amazing. We ate in Chinatown for lunch and drank wine for two hours. Staring into his eyes, which I think are really beautiful, I really did feel as if I could lose myself. We went to Fisherman's Wharf and he bought me a rose. That made me nervous because it kind of officially made it a date instead of the bullshit buying sneakers excuse we had first used for our trip to SF.

"I'm happy for you," Lisa said. "Just be careful. There's so much that's new right now in our lives. I'm not sure I trust him yet, Sharon. Take your time."

I hear you Lisa. It's just that our feelings are so powerful, and it's on some kind of innate level. With Matthew and Morrow. But keep giving me the loving reality checks. I appreciate them.

December 1, 1986 • Another happening that really helps get me through the day around here is the small singing group some of us 1Ls have formed. We call ourselves Just Friends. Ben, a brother from Miami, is actually simultaneously getting his law degree and a master's in business; he has such a beautiful voice. He got the group rolling. And there is Rowland from St. Kitts, who is our committed and staunch director, along with our small, dedicated group. We have begun to practice together. We were one soprano short, however, until we met Krista.

Ben had heard that Krista could sing. He grabbed me on the way to torts one day and told me there was a woman in there who could really sing and would be great for the group. We stood peeking in the torts door before class started, with Ben searching until he spotted Krista. "There she is," he said, "that white girl with the white hair." When I looked, I saw that her hair was literally white, bleached in this incredible, funky, short, asymmetrical haircut that made me yearn for the Village back home in New York. I liked her instantly. As it turns out, she can really sing, or "sang," as we say, gospel style.

We are going to sing at the Law School Coffeehouse. Rowland, who knows his stuff, and the group say I can really "sang." After years of being in the chorus in college and high school and singing solos in front of my mirror at home, one of my dreams is coming true. I am a soloist!

December 16, 1986 • I'm leaving to go home for Christmas in the next few days and to study for finals, which will occur after the holiday break, not like some law schools, which give finals before the holidays. I am excited to go home and feel as though I have lived a lot of life in these past four months.

Lisa and I have gotten to be close friends so quickly. I remember Mommy saying before I left that I wouldn't find the kind of lasting friendships in law school that I did in college, because in college we were in essence "still growing up" together. I guess her point was that lasting friendships are formed while you are in those growing-up years and not beyond. I think she is wrong. My friendship with Lisa is lasting; I know it is. And while we don't have the history that I have with my best college friends, we are building new history together.

In fact, we are learning and growing. I feel us becoming young women and leaving girlhood behind and supporting each other in this transition. Every time I start thinking I am all grown up and an adult, I realize that I am still evolving. Lisa said in a note recently that we grow more loving as we get older. I think that is a very insightful point, but I would add: When we let ourselves. We have new men in our lives, new school, new state. Everything is new, except us, striving to maintain our sense of self amid the changes. We find in each other soulmates, unconditional acceptance, friendship, and pure fun.

January 26, 1987 • Lisa and I found a dark corner on the third floor of the law school, down from the library, a corner you wouldn't know was there unless you looked really hard to find it. We sat on the floor, close to each other, kind of staring out into space. The new semester is just beginning, and we grabbed a quiet moment just to sit.

I opened my grades, I said slowly. I did fine in my other three classes, but, I might as well just come out and say this, I got an R in civil procedure. I know it's not an F, but it's one small step away.

Sometimes we have what we call Dumb Days, days when we feel we just aren't getting it. Days when all you have to say is, "I'm having a Dumb Day." We call them Dumb Days because it is a way of labeling the day and the moment and not ourselves, of allowing ourselves the space to acknowledge a moment of fear or lack of knowledge, while maintaining our sense of humor, and sharing our vulnerabilities. It is a way of talking to someone who feels safe. And, of course, of instantly knowing how the other person is feeling. An invaluable gift to each other and to ourselves, Dumb Days are a new experience for us, a gift of law school.

We have developed ways to cope with and to ride out a Dumb Day. I think that's part of many a person's law school experience, except they don't want to admit it. Maybe you could even extend that to life. Forget about calling it a Dumb Day, but call it a day when everything just doesn't add up and make sense, no matter how many times you compute it. Yet it just is.

Thing with Lisa is, when I have one of those days, I can really talk to her about it, without censure or embarrassment or apology. Lisa usually gets over a Dumb Day pretty quickly. I think deep down inside she has a centeredness, an ability to see beyond the meaning or lack of meaning in the moment. She has perspective, I guess you'd call it.

The irony is, lately, the more days that pass, and the more experiences we have, we've started to realize that sometimes maybe it's not really us having a Dumb Day. Perhaps the questions…and answers we have are legitimate and real; we simply have to voice them.

Lisa believes in me even when I doubt myself; the doubting myself part is another new experience. She has begun to say that our voices, our respective "takes on things," might be different from many other voices of law students, but that our voices have a power and strength all their own. Different life experiences naturally result in different voices, or viewpoints. All we need to do is allow ourselves to speak.

So hanging out in that corner, weighing on my mind, was the grade I had received in civil procedure. OK, it was an R for restricted credit, the essential equivalent of a D. I have not been one to sweat grades in life. The great, the good, or the bad, and I have received all of the above. But I felt really bad and ashamed of this grade, and I'd told none of my classmates, not even other best friends. But I knew I could tell Lisa. So I did.

When I did, she told it to me straight. "Who you are is not your grade Sharon. You are Sharon, and all that goes into being you. All those things I love about you and all those ways in which you are growing and learning to be a stronger you. OK, that's your grade for this course. It is what it is. It's not the end of your law school career. It just is. And now it's a new semester, with new classes, new chances, and new grades. You can do it. Accept it. Let it go. Move on to . . . today."

Lisa didn't lie and say it wasn't a bad grade. It just was. She has this unique way of helping you to accept truths while searching inside of yourself for the brightest parts of who you are. She helped me do that today; me, who feel as though it is usually my role to help others. Lisa is one of the first people in my adult life whom I truly feel I can lean on. And leaning, really leaning doesn't come to me easy, but I know her small five-foot self can shoulder the weight.

February 3, 1987 • Lisa is wrestling with her relationship with her dude. I can sure relate to that, since Matthew and I certainly have our moments as we discover each other. I have a feeling with this guy; Lisa is in uncharted territory. Still she handles it with the panache and honesty with which she approaches everything. I love our friendship.

Yesterday she said, "Little Sharon, help! I'm all confused, a victim of my hormones. Do you think (1) I can hang out with him as long as he keeps his hands off me, or do I (2) need to stay away from him altogether, forever?"

Lisa, I told her, giving her a dose of Sharon plainspeak, which I guess is part of why we make such good friends, you are walking a really fine line. I would say yes to one, but that is probably because I am a gambler. The ultimate sensible thing to do would be two. But who ever said we were sensible?

"Sharon, you are such a pal. Thank goodness you understand and don't criticize me. I really appreciate the fact that I can tell you everything and know you'll still love me. I can't be perfect. Number two wouldn't really solve anything because the potential for number one would always be there."

Lisa, I said, I love you, too.

February 11, 1986 • For me, the highlight of our new schedule of courses is constitutional law, with Professor Paul Brest. This is a course I can sink my teeth into. I am really starting to speak up. My confidence is growing in my right to express my opinions, whether similar to or different from those of the majority, or of the professor, for that matter. Dumb Days are lessening. (There are still plenty of them for all of us in property, a course we discuss so abstractly that I forget what subject we are talking about.)

Right now in class we are talking about the origins of constitutional law, specifically, how and why the earliest cases were decided and how large a role politics and the struggle for power between the Federalists and the Republicans played in the Supreme Court's decision-making process and how the Court determined its jurisdiction. I find it so intriguing to finally be in a class where (at least for these early cases in the 1700s and early 1800s) it is acknowledged that part of why a case turned this way or that way was the agenda of the judge and the times. Judges are, after all, human beings. This notion that somehow a judge is a true arbiter of objectivity, or that the law itself is, makes less and less sense to me the more I learn. Sometimes it seems that in general, the world, and most especially some professors and students, act as if the black letter law is the equivalent of Moses' Ten Commandments. Carved in stone. That hallowed and that holy.

Today I spoke in class. I said that I believe the law is a valuable and essential element of organized society, but that doesn't mean there are not laws that are inequitable, inadequate, or wrong. Even the Constitution, which originally granted no voting rights to women and blacks, is obviously not without its "problems." So why do we sometimes study all this stuff as if it is supposed to be inherently right or that it makes sense?

We are also taking a class called lawyering process that is supposed to teach us a lot more about what it is like to be real lawyers. I'm not sure I like it. That's OK. I didn't come here just to be a lawyer, anyway. This may sound corny, but I came here because I wanted to understand what makes this country tick, to learn more about the power structure of this nation and to study the law and how I can make a positive difference. Also, I wanted to challenge myself academically and to always have a guarantee of food on the table. The jury is certainly out . . . smile. Anyway, I digress.

What I do like, is that lawyering process class provides a dose of everything from mediation to negotiation to litigation. I love mediation. When we mediate, it's all about trying to make all the parties come out of a conflict feeling as whole as possible. I guess that is a lot more me. Still, we've got Moot Court coming up, arguing in its finest form. There's a winner and a loser. That's just the way it goes. I don't like getting caught up in that type of competition. Still, I am learning something in the process, and I really like my Moot Court partner, Roni.

February 20, 1987 • Lisa was sad today. When I asked her what was up, she shared it with me in that matter-of-fact way of hers.

"You know I graduated from Harvard the year before you graduated BU? Well, I had two best friends there, Lydia and Erin. I guess you could call us kind of a three musketeer crew. I mean, we were that close. After graduation, Erin and I stayed in Massachusetts, and Lydia moved to New York. Last year, right around this time, Lydia was raped and thrown off the roof of her apartment."

I sucked in my breath. I'd never expected her to say that.

"They say people could hear her screaming, but no one helped her."

It's strange, but the way Lisa shared it so straight and to the point somehow intensified the moment and the pain.

It was so hard to find the words to say. Sitting there with Lisa, I hoped she could feel my love and sorrow. I can't imagine how horrible she must have felt to lose her beloved best friend.

February 26, 1987 • School is really heating up. The stakes are getting higher. You can feel it. It is interview season for first-years. There are only 175 first-years, but more than 500 law firms have or will come to interview us for summer jobs. There are five black women in our class. Besides me, two of the other black women are from New York.

It is funny because although all three of us are very different, we have become very close friends. Lena seemed quiet and restrained before I got to know her; Gina is just the opposite. Then there's me somewhere in the middle.

There have been no "call-backs" yet to speak of for us from our job interviews. It is starting to really get to us. We've formed the "unofficial" black woman's no-job-yet club to support each other. Gina makes some great jokes about it. I guess we all do to keep ourselves going. Lisa, who is Jewish, is an honorary member. Catherine, my roommate, who has call-backs flying out of her ears, is a loving supporter. We make quite a team. We're keeping our chins up.

Check this out, I've got to save this one. It's a note Lisa and I were writing to each other in our law and economics class. Our notes, sometimes funny, painful, encouraging, or brutal home truths, have become a part of us here.

Lisa: I think this on-campus interview shit sucks, and I really do think they don't want to hire black women. Law firms suck. I told one guy he had too many pictures of white men in his firm resume. Gutsy, huh?

Me: Wow (I wrote a new poem yesterday while in Property. I call it "Black Woman in a Sometimes NonBlack Woman World."

Lisa: Being a woman can be tough in general also, and you have both. But at least you're smart and beautiful.

March 5, 1987 • Last Friday was hysterical. Lisa won the "Dress for Mediocrity" contest that Dean Ely threw to lift our first-year spirits. Dressed in lace stockings and a black skirt, with her hair pinned high on her head, she won the category Least Likely to Get a Corporate Job. She loved it.

We have a black professor in the law school! He is Professor Charles Lawrence, a learned scholar of impressive credentials who is also really down to earth. Lena has him for constitutional law. So far so good . . . I hope to take education law with him next semester. It is a very small class, and the competition is fierce to be selected. You have to write an essay on why you want to take this course. I also finally got the story on what happened with last year's constitutional law professor, at least, some folks' version of it. It seems he was a constitutional law professor and scholar from Harvard, teaching at Stanford as a visiting professor for the semester, that being common in law schools for professors to serve as visiting profs at other institutions. He was teaching first-year constitutional law.

Some of the students assigned to his section began feeling he couldn't teach the class (as in like he didn't know what he was talking about, I guess) and that they weren't learning the subject. They actually started attending the other two constitutional law sections, in essence boycotting the professor's class. There was a lot of talk disparaging of his teaching until finally BLSA students stood in front of the class and read a public statement that decried what was occurring. At that point the school administration finally stepped in and put a stop to what should never have been permitted to happen. The students returned to their rightfully assigned classes, and the professor's name was added to the long list of renowned blacks who experience disrespect and pressure and carry on.

March 15, 1987 • It's late winter, which feels like midsummer for those of us used to the cold of the Northeast.

Lisa's little sister, Merrill, has come out to visit. Lisa and Merrill are a two-girl family, two years apart, just like Sherry and me. One more thing we have in common. Sherry is scheduled to come out to visit next month.

This morning Lisa and her sister rented a car and were going out for a day of horseback riding and swimming. Catherine and I were on our way to the library when we bumped into them, getting ready to pull off. I stuck my face in the passenger window, my arm resting on the door. "Come on Sharon, come with us," they said, laughing and teasing and trying to pull me inside.

I, ever ready for a good time with my friends, took a full minute to think about blowing off my work and jumping in the car and stopping at my trailer for a swimsuit.

No, I can't do it, I said, not because of my work, but because of singing rehearsal with our gospel group Just Friends this evening. I knew I'd never make it back in time.

March 16, 1987 • Morning, and I was lying in bed, although it was time for constitutional law. I was thinking about how Lisa was going to yell at me if I skipped class, when the phone rang.

Lisa's roommate was on the phone, telling me that yesterday evening on the way to the stables, a drunk driver crashed into Lisa's car.

Her sister was injured. Lisa was killed.

My little Lisa?

Killed.

March 18, 1987 • How do we make sense of death?

Or perhaps, more important, how do we ascertain the meaning of a life?

The only way to sooth my spirit is to write about Lisa.

At the memorial ceremony for Lisa, I offered the words below. They mean so much to me, to Lisa and me, and to our beliefs. They also explain, at least in part, how I interpret life and self in the context of the surreal world of Stanford.

These words held me as I loved them into a poem.

LISA,

I talk with you in my mind. Yet I look for you at school
Your smile lights my day. Yet you have gone away
I can't seem to understand that you are not here
So maybe that's not true. A part of you is with us always
Sharing, laughing and being sarcastic or blunt, as you call it
Something I always teased you about.
You know Little Lisa,
Every time I try to understand that you are gone
My head feels like it's on crooked
And I'm left trying to hold it on straight
And yet still understand the world
So maybe the world isn't meant to be understood.
I'm so glad we took the time to be friends
I'm so glad we took the time to laugh and talk

I'm so glad we gave the time to share our lives
Even if there was something we really had to do
It got done
But only after we were people first
Because in the end that's all that really matters
So you know, baby, there's so much I could tell you right now
But you probably know it already anyway. You always do
Thank you for being a wonderful friend
For loving and caring and being sane
In a place occasionally gone mad
Thanks for giving me a kick or a hug
When you knew that's what I needed
I think about all our good times
Like chick night or talking about our little sisters all the time
Or my coming to lay my problems at your door
And you always making me be honest with myself
Or writing notes in class
Or twirling our hair at each other like we used to do
And I thank God for the gift that is you
So yeah, Lis, right now I'm being a crybaby
You know, like I can be sometimes
But I know you'd say
It's OK, Little Sharon
Because I still love you anyway

Lisa was the only person who ever called me Little Sharon. Even though she was only five feet and I stand five feet five, the affection of that name meant the world to me.

At Lisa's memorial, our group Just Friends sang "Lean On Me," in her honor. We held each other up, standing close together with arms encircling each others waists, and sang.

Our civil procedure teacher read Lisa's law school admission essay. It was so beautiful, incredibly well written, and profound that it blew everybody away, even me, who knew her so well. What Lisa wore on her sleeve was not her intellect or her grade-point average, although she was a Harvard graduate and an accomplished flautist.

What she shared above all was her essence. There for anyone to see and experience was her spirit, the authentic Lisa. It takes courage to share your essence, and to do so in the unequivocal and courageous way she did. The professor also said she'd gotten an A in his class. That was Lisa.

One of her best friends, Lawrence—Lisa always says his name Law-rence—also spoke at the ceremony. He shared, "She cared so much about the people around her. One of our very first conversations was about what she thought was her greatest handicap—and what I believe was her greatest asset—that she would open up to others to the point of vulnerability. But how could we experience life without saying what we feel or being willing to become dependent upon the people around us? I am very sad today because of a selfish wish that we could go running again or hang out and skip studying for the day, but I'm not sad for Lisa. She wanted the most out of today, and I hope she got it . . ."

A drunk driver cut Lisa's life short. She died almost instantly. A woman, a passerby, held her hand as she softly moaned, her sister Merrill, who survived the accident, unconscious beside her. I am so thankful for that woman who held my friend's hand and shared her warmth as Lisa took her last breaths. Still, somehow, in my silent moments, it is as if I can hear Lisa's quiet sigh. But greater than the sound of any soft breath is the music that she made while she lived.

THE DAY LISA DIED WAS THE DAY I PROMISED MYSELF TO ALWAYS LIVE MY LIFE LOVING, FIRST.

The week before Lisa's death, when we were walking from our lockers weighted down with heavy casebooks, she talked about how you never know how you are going to die, so you've got to truly live. She said it very matter-of-factly, the way she said most things. I thought about that conversation after her death. Yes Lisa, you're right, and as I travel this journey, doggedly continuing past the juncture where we were permanently forced to part, I strive to always keep those words in mind.

LISTENING TO MUSIC OF SURVIVAL
I have sucked in air
Crafting lyrics in my mind
That sing a tune
Never far from lips
Open to a world
That may or may not
Kiss back.

Pack Love

I KNEW AFTER THE DAY LISA WAS TAKEN FROM US, with a surety that would survive even the pain, that I've got to live my life like this, now and forever. If I'd never gotten to know Lisa, I would have missed something so precious no GPA could ever replace it.

So then, as I went on, finishing finals without her, sitting in class without her and ultimately graduating without her, the lesson of loving first and the power of that message has never waned. I wear her gold scarf sometimes for good luck or good feeling. Years later, when my apartment was broken into and my jewelry stolen, they stole Lisa's earrings that her parents had given me in her memory. But they didn't get the scarf, and they didn't get the memories.

There are many things that Stanford was, as an experience. I share them along the journey. But surprisingly enough, if you think that what I learned foremost was the law, well, that's just not true. What I learned was about myself, and about life, about making choices as to who we are and how we want to travel this journey.

Losing Lisa was also a lesson in finding the adult me, validating who we were and who I am still.

My learning of the law and critical thinking and all the rest matters, too. But who we are as people is what matters to me first.

Even after all these years, as I write these words, the pain still strikes me. But it really happened, and she's gone . . . from this earth anyway . . . never from our hearts. I think about all the life

I have lived since those moments we last shared, and it feels like a lifetime in and of itself. Perhaps it is. I think of all the things I've experienced that we used to dream or joke about, and all the things I never imagined could happen, that did.

But then we didn't know any of this. We had just begun a new chapter in our lives.

Our first year of Stanford Law School, and it was a long journey there, for both of us.

And so, I place love in my bag. I vow to never take it out to make space for other items, or think I can leave it on the shelf for a time and pick up some more on the road. Because it's true that love is one of those valuables I know I never want to be without. I always want to have more than enough to share with those along the way, on my life's journey.

9

Keep On Steppin' Because You Have Learned the Value of Your Own Two Feet

July 7, 1987 • Staring out the window as the big city bus whizzes down the street in the summer sun. The air conditioning is working way overtime and doing the job of an overachiever. Though I no longer see the tall man or some of the other people Sherry and I used to make up stories about along the way, the bus route is the same and parts of me are as well. Then again, the course of time has brought much change, many things I never dreamed would happen and, of course, many events I'd hoped and prayed for. And I am grown up and can't go back. I can see little Sharon and Sherry sitting eagerly in their seats waiting to arrive at Hillside Avenue, the many mornings of snow or springtime, or running to not be late to school.

Now, I am on my way to work.

July 8, 1987 • What an eye opener—working for the New York Lawyers For The Public Interest. After a year of studying the law, I get to experience it in action.

The lawyers here have me working on a housing case of secondary displacement, a class action lawsuit to help people that live in "Hell's Kitchen" here in the city. It's the only home they know, and the goal is to keep a roof over their heads.

This is certainly the other end of the spectrum from the legal theory and study we've been doing all year. I labor on with the legal research necessary to bring this suit to court and to fight to win . . . or at least to hold off the inevitable defeat it sometimes seems the veteran lawyers anticipate.

July 9, 1987 • I've been reading the depositions and testimonies of the residents of the apartments, telling of all kinds of experiences that, before now, I've witnessed only on television. Of people hired to intimidate them out of their residences, fires set and residents beaten. And of nowhere to go. I'm really thankful this is the work I am doing this summer. At the same time, it is occasionally tough to separate my emotions from the cool legal head necessary to conduct research and draft a legal memo to achieve results for our clients.

I'm learning so much they don't tell you in law school. Maybe they can't tell you because you have to live it and see it for yourself . . . See the law at work or when it doesn't work. The lawyers here have all kind of stories of experiences they've had over the years.

Working with lawyers really dedicated to helping people feels like coming home, not just to New York, but to a place where I can bring my heart and mind and soul to work.

I am so glad I got this job.

The New York Lawyers For The Public Interest is one of the best public interest law firms in the country. And they've achieved all kinds of positive results in making a difference for people in education, civil rights and a host of other areas. Since I've been interviewing with public interest organizations, I've found that what I have to offer is highly valued—so unlike my experiences with corporate law firms. Deep.

The pay certainly isn't the same as in corporate America and what my classmates are making, but what I am experiencing in my spirit is priceless. Lisa would be proud. I won the Lisa Schnitzer Public Interest Scholarship at Stanford established by Lisa's family this year. Using the scholarship money that enables me to live this summer, doing this work, I am struck by the irony, the beauty and the bitter sweetness of this world. Lisa would know exactly what I mean.

July 10, 1987 • Today, I allow myself the release of my words, inspired by a particularly painful deposition I read of one of our clients.

IF I GO CRAZY
Send me to a place
Where music is the dominant sound
Don't let me stay here
Where silence is golden,
But no gold paves the streets
Where, instead, the streets
Are streaked with dirt, and tears, and pain
But they keep telling you
That the gold is simply inlaid in the tar
And you're not looking in the right place
And you're not bending low enough to spot it
Or reaching far enough to pick up the prize
Or working hard enough to deserve it,
This precious substance, illusory in its beauty
For all it is
Is cold metal,
So even if gold does pave the streets

And I am among the many
Who simply don't have the right color eyes
To detect its reflecting glint,
I don't need its inflexible, icy beauty
I'm going crazy
And a place where music
is the dominant sound
Where beauty is soft and soulful
rhythmic and deep,
Is infinitely more preferable
To this.

July 17, 1987 • Last week I was walking down Fourteenth Street in my bright tight yellow legging pants with the thin yellow suspenders. I was coming back from researching at NYU library. Dreaming as usual. Up the street, a lean wiry black woman was going down the street swinging her arms randomly, her hands tightly balled into fists, as a tourist-looking white family quickly moved out of her way.

I didn't see her until it was too late. She landed a punch to my esophagus that would still ache two days later. I couldn't believe it.

No one said anything. I went to a payphone and called my job to tell them what happened and reach out to someone. The receptionist, who is also from Jamaica Queens, answered the phone.

Listening to my story, she said, "Girl, didn't you grow up in Rochdale Village? You should have gotten out of the way. You should know better than that."

Thanks for the sympathy I said. I sucked it up, rubbed my throat, and played it off, rejoining the throng of New Yorkers rushing down the dry, sun-cracked street. One week later, I walked by this guy on the street in Midtown. "She got stars in her eyes," he exclaimed.

I've started wearing shades.

August 15, 1987 • It's almost time to return to school. I can't believe how fast it's gone by. Sherry is moving back to New York from her job in Boston, to start working in film, ironically right when I am leaving to go back to California. It's wild how our lives are going so quickly and so much is happening. I am thankful for our glorious sisterhood and for the fact that no matter how many miles separate us, we are tied together by our love and by our bouk-a-shouk.

Getting ready to go back to Stanford. The class action law suit continues, so I won't get to see it through. It could go on for years; that's the way it is sometimes with the law.

I've done some powerful soul searching. As I begin second year, I am trying to figure out what all this stuff really means. Study. Practice. Living. Goals. What's it all about? I am in law school because I really want to make a positive difference in this world. And I want to help even those good ol' scales of justice, so often in need of an adjustment. My Dumb Days are fading. Fading as I come on stronger . . . by forging on. . . . Carrying the banner and believing in who I am and what I am here to do. Working this summer showed me that some of my opinions expressed in classes are more valid than I thought. Law school needs varied perspectives. I am going to begin speaking up more, as I have been doing for most of my life. I don't have to be silent. Because I believe in what I am saying.

October 6, 1987 • *Second Year, First Semester*
"Sharon, did you hear that Patricia Williams is coming to give a lecture?" Gina ran up to me after immigration law, effervescent as always. No, who is she? I asked. "She's a preeminent law scholar and professor. And a black woman."

A black woman professor coming to speak! I am so excited.

Obviously a lot of other people are, too. A few days later her guest lecture was packed when we arrived.

As I sat listening to her lecture, her voice and words were poetry, law and sheer brilliance combined. All of a sudden, sitting there, it occurred to me that I, too, could be a law professor.

And I understand now why I haven't thought before about being a law professor, because there was no black woman I could look to. No reflection of me. Now I've got another choice. An option I always had but never knew.

Professor Williams actually incorporates her poetry into her analysis. And it's OK to do that. It is brilliant. I am inspired.

Right around the time of my October 6, 1987 entry, I lost my beloved journal.

In coming home to New York for a visit, the suitcase with my journal in it got left on the sidewalk as we unloaded the car.

Imagine my devastation when I lost it, not only because of how precious it was to me, but also because of how personal. I lost it right in front of our building. Mommy and Sherry left our apartment and looked everywhere for the bag.

But it was gone.

At first I cried and cried. I was devastated. Gradually I calmed down, reminding myself that the memories were in my heart and the poetry memorized in my mind. I could write the poems down again, and no loss could ever erase my journey. It took quite awhile to get over it. But in that time, I didn't do any journal writing.

However, what I did write was a piece called "Reflections" for my class in constitutional law, minority issues with Professor Chuck Lawrence. It is a reflection piece on some of my experiences at Stanford. Ironically, it shares a pivotal portion of my journey during this time. I believe it spells out, as plainly as my journal, some of the experiences and insights I explored at this particular juncture of my journey.

I think it's a pretty gutsy paper, at times quite angry and frustrated and in other instances reflective and celebratory. But perhaps, above all, it is real and it is raw as to where I was at and how I worked to hang in there to grow to the next step . . . to truly come into my own and to reach my goal of being able to powerfully give and help others. Sharon, shedding the last vestiges of her child skin and becoming a woman.

Reflections Piece • Constitutional Law, Minority Issues

REFLECTIONS
Whispers
Soft curls of sound, words barely discerned
Whisper in my ear
Soothing in their rhythm
They are so feather light
It is not even necessary
To know their meaning.

Trying to Make Sense of My Law School Journey

Perhaps if I could have existed, listening only to sweet soft sounds whispering soothingly in my ear, I would not have had to hear the jarring notes of dissonance . . . alas, also known as reality.

Do I wish this were so? That I could hear light whispers and shut my ears to the rest? I guess not. Although it is a hard call right now. The way I am feeling.

After all, I keep thinking, that's why I came to Stanford Law School; I wanted to figure out just what the loud blaring notes were that I kept hearing. They were so rhythmless. I felt sure if I could just understand how the notes fit together, I would hear the music and comprehend its meaning and its rhythm.

Certainly now, after a few years here, I know the music, recognize the lyrics, and can even hum a bar or two (perhaps more) if required. But there is little joy in the knowledge, except literally for the joy of knowledge, of comprehension. I do believe there is strength within true understanding of reality. Although I reserve the right to remain an idealist . . . for in ideals, lie hope.

In Emily Dickinson's poem "Emancipation," she says:
Captivity is consciousness.
So's liberty.

It is true that I have found liberty within myself these past few years. And for that I rejoice.

I am thinking of wonderfully passionate liberating moments snatched amid the constant (when I chose to make it so) task of digesting case books, notes, articles, theories, answers, analysis, laws, rules, standards, insults, slaps in the face, discourse, dialogue, memos and pain.

There is the moment when I discover Alice Walker's description of the word "womanist," and I can cry, "Yes, that's me!"

Womanist

Encompasses "feminist" as it is defined in Webster's, but also means instinctively pro-woman. It is not in the dictionary at all. Nonetheless, it has a strong root in Black women's culture. It comes (to me) from the word "womanish" a word our mothers used to describe, and attempt to inhibit strong, outrageous, or outspoken behavior when we were children: "You're acting womanish!" A label that failed, for the most part to keep us from acting "womanish" whenever we could, that is to say, like our mothers themselves, and like other women we admired.

An advantage to using womanist is that, because it is from my own culture I needn't preface it with the word Black (an awkward necessity and a problem I have with the word feminist), since Blackness is implicit in the term; just as for white women, there is apparently no felt need to preface feminist with the word "white," since the word feminist is accepted as coming out of white women's culture.

The lesson and beauty of this word *womanist* give me something permanent to hold, definitive, tangible. I can write the word in the palm of my hand, grasp it and know it is indelibly stamped there even when the ink has faded.

A few years ago the term *womanist* would have meant next to nothing to me. Had I heard it, I would have comprehended its meaning, but my spirit certainly would not have responded. *Feminist* would also have rung hollow, except perhaps (as Alice Walker's description states) to make me think of a white woman talking about ideas to which I could not necessarily relate.

My consciousness centered around myself first as a person, and then as a black person. I was raised with a strong racial identity and always prided myself on this. I never realized there might be more to my identity than being black . . . namely, being a woman.

Fitting In or Out

When I arrived at Stanford Law School, I immediately got involved in the Black Law Students Association. As co-chair of BLSA's Political Social Change Committee, I was dealing with the multitude of issues that affect us as blacks in this community. I was sensitive and in tune to instances of racism for both blacks and other people of color in various venues such as class, textbooks, and professors.

I attended the Women of Stanford Law Potluck at the beginning of the year. I was surprised to find that it felt different to be in a group of solely women when we had gotten together for this express purpose. Somehow it felt unifying, although to a limited degree. I didn't feel that I could "identify" all that well with some of the women there, but I realized that I still felt more of a sense of belonging than I did when I was with these women and their male counterparts in the same room.

(Are there, indeed, male counterparts for women? When I phrased it that way I was thinking of white, male law students [let's say a heterosexual, upper class, Ivy League educated type] and a woman of the same background. But is this woman his mirror image beyond superficial traits? I think not, but that's not to say many a woman of this description would not herself disagree with me. I believe her experiences as a woman has to lend her some insight via experience of oppression through sexism. The real question is, simply, does she label it as such?)

Nonetheless, one area to which I definitely had not given much thought was sexism and the oppression of women. I admit that I had fallen prey to the dreaded ranking of oppressions. Although in all honesty, were I forced to rank oppressions, racism would outrank sexism, at least in this country. (I recall this conversation in our constitutional law, minority issues class. It was a painful discussion for us all. I doubt however, that I made this admission at that time regarding sexism and racism.)

But that is not the point. It should not be the point. And now I am forced to confess anger toward myself for alluding to the comparison. But still I'll let the statement remain in this writing, so I guess I must find it not ultimately problematic.

Sympathy vs. Empathy, United By Our Issues As Women

I remember, first year, many women in our criminal law class were upset by the professor's handling of discussions of women as victims of such attacks as rape and domestic violence. Although I was sympathetic to these women who felt such pain during class dialogues—note the word dialogue is used here sarcastically because the professor's handling of it did not feel that way at all—I didn't empathize. There is such a huge difference between empathy and sympathy. To me it is the difference between relating, touching, and simply looking on, perhaps with sadness or pity in one's eyes and heart.

Why couldn't I empathize? I was not awakened enough to realize that all my sisters' concerns should be my own. Not just because their pain should be shared by me, although certainly it should, but also because threats and pain experienced by some women are threats against us all. No woman is immune to the threat or fear of rape. Ignorance is one's only immunity. No immunity could be more illusory than that.

Men's and Women's Voices

Now I'm thinking back to my lawyering process class. One day we discussed the concept of the difference between men and women's voices. I don't participate much. Why, I can't really say. Maybe I was just digesting the information.

I thought about how I spoke in class, really how I expressed myself in general. I didn't feel like I spoke the same as many of the others in my small section who now seemed to bark nothing but legal jargon. Usually, I had to sift through their comments at length to arrive at the "point." I noticed how much more frequently women prefaced their remarks with "I think," "I feel," or "I believe."

Still, the real point goes far beyond those surface identifications. Robin West's article "Economic Man and Literary Woman: One Contrast" expresses some aspects of this phenomenon wonderfully. She discusses economic man's commitment to being rational:

He relentlessly chooses what he prefers, prefers what he wants, wants what he desires, and desires what will maximize his subjective well-being. He is perfectly rational.

In contrast, West describes the literary woman:

Her character is multimotivational, which is why it is worth explor-
ing, and she does not know herself—her own subjectivity as well as
she might. . . . She is sufficiently complex so that as a character, she is
worth portraying, and as a reader she is worthy of dialogue, she is
educable.

To me, Robin West's descriptions are strongly reminiscent of how men and women at SLS often interact. That is not to say there are not men and women who fall into both categories. Even then, those men with more of a "literary" bent, using West's description, are frequently likely to be men of color, gay or from a lower economic bracket. I cannot believe this is happenstance.

Getting Acquainted With Sexism

I noticed as the months progressed that my voice—I mean by the word "voice" what I had to say and how I said it—was different and more unique than the voices of the majority. That is not to say that my voice has more or less weight than other voices. Each must judge voices for him or herself, or so they tell me. It reminds me of what my friend Lisa was talking about first year. The value of each voice. Including our own. She got it. Then.

However, I couldn't figure out why it was that when I made a statement I felt to be important or profound, comments made to me after class consisted of such remarks as, "Don't you look pretty today," "I love your hair," or "What a beautiful color blouse."

I don't mind compliments, but these hurt. It took me awhile to realize this was because the remarks replaced comments on my insights and who I am. Instead they focused upon the superficiality of what I look like. It took even longer to discern that this type of treatment was none other than that mysterious word I'd thought so little about . . . sexism.

What I had to say in class seemed to be given little weight. Finally it dawned on me that it wasn't that my comments were so off base (which I'd begun to fear they were), but that many people simply did not wish to listen to a different point of view from a diverse experiential base. As this realization grew, I began to become more "aware" and more "angry."

I wrote this poem while sitting in property class:

> *I don't care if I'm a black woman*
> *In a non-black woman world*
> *Within my mind, and body, and soul*
> *It still feels good.*

The use of the word woman in this poem took on new meaning, more meaning than had I written black "person." I was beginning to define and value the beauty of being a woman as well as the value and beauty in being black, although I had yet to combine these two aspects of "self" into one cohesive whole.

I've always been a woman who loves and enjoys being with other women. But I'd never given my women friends much thought in the sense of exactly what helped us relate or bond together . . . namely being women. That is clearly not to say that this is the sole reason, but falling back upon my ever present racial analogy, I know that often friendships with other minorities are expanded by our shared experiences. Certainly the same is true with our status as women.

Cleaning and Housekeeping
Recollections of an awakening:

I am in an interview for a first-year summer job with a Los Angeles corporate law firm. I sit suitably stiffly and professionally in my navy pinstripe suit (which I think is perfect for the occasion but friends will painfully tell me the following year . . . is too tight . . . for corporate America anyway).

This is perhaps my tenth interview of the season. No callbacks. I tell the relatively young, white male associate about myself. Articulately, concisely and what I think is reasonable "economic mannish."

I guess not. For when in answer to his question, "What can I tell you about our firm?" I say, "What exactly would a summer law clerk do?" He responds, "Cleaning and housekeeping."

"Then I must be in the wrong place," I say. "Oh, excuse me, that wasn't really appropriate of me," he states, ending the exchange. (I could talk about what happened next after I did report this experience—the policy SLS had in place to handle this discriminatory interview or how I, the victim, became by necessity a leader and agitator in the struggle to strengthen the policy, or how this experience further politicized me, or the way this particular struggle for a better policy continues now . . .)

I walk out after the knock that heralds the next interviewee's arrival. I am conscious of the racism of the experience. But it is not until we are walking home that my boyfriend, Matthew, pushing his bike beside me, points out to me the unique status of the remark. The interviewer would not have said this to a black man or a white woman; this type of abuse is reserved for women of color.

At first I resist the notion; I don't know why. Perhaps I did not wish to feel segregated from blackness, put into a special category I'd never really considered: that of black women. I didn't want to admit that I could be different (and let's face it, devalued) in comparison to the black man who had preceded me into that interviewer's room.

Gradually, though, the truth begins to sink into my consciousness. The submersion is long and painful, yet there is joy in the experience, too—the joy of being a black woman. I love being a black woman, with all the baggage that may come with this life. I wouldn't trade my black womaness for anything else. I love my brown skin and, although I have a love/hate war with my hair, I confess I'd miss it if I couldn't cornrow it and know it would stay!

Looking in the Mirror

Further recollection:

It is second year. I am sitting dejectedly in the Women of Stanford Law office, fighting back tears. It's interviewing season again and the ratio of interviews to callbacks (or lack thereof) is wearing on my emotional stability and self-esteem.

Just then the door opens and in bounces a woman classmate of mine. Blonde and blue-eyed, she has a reputation in our class as a person with a decided lack of empathy. Nonetheless, I've never had anything particularly against her, and when she asks me jauntily, "How's it going?" I don't bother to deny that it's going "shittily."

She begins to talk to me about her interview experience and how the opposite is true for her. She then explains to me her take on "why."

"When an interviewer sits behind his desk and looks at me, he sees his daughter or his wife twenty years ago. I see my father . . . and we know exactly how to talk to each other," she says.

There is no apology or introspection to her explanation. It simply is. And yet I do not take offense. Yes, I am different. I'd never thought about it in quite these terms before. I never would have imagined that the man behind the desk was my father.

But de facto, this conversation necessitates introspection for me. I have no choice. Therein lies a telling difference between us. She has thought about the "why" for herself, anyway, but not the many whys beneath the surface. I wonder if she's thought what it means that an interviewer can see in her his daughter, but not his son . . . and all the differences this dichotomy represents. Does she care?

She tells me the story of an interview, where the interviewer asks her, "What excites you?" She replies, "Money." I am grossed out. But she tells me he loved it. I take her word for it.

She bounces out the door, casually throwing a *good luck* over her shoulder.

Although grossed out with her account, when I finally get a callback to fly to visit a firm and interview with a cutthroat partner type, I find myself remembering her words. I would be working half the summer at a public interest law firm in Los Angeles, but this was my last chance to find a corporate job for the other half of the summer, important to me because I needed the money and wanted the experience.

I felt this man would hate who Sharon Simpson is; I tried, for once, to be the opposite of her. When he asked me what I want most out of life, the answer that immediately popped into my head was love and happiness. Sounds sappy, but it's true. I knew I couldn't tell him this, so I threw back my head, tossed my hair, bared my teeth and boldly replied, "Success and money." Even he was taken aback, and tried to make me back down. Of course I didn't. I figured out that was part of the game and that, in reality, I'd expressed his desires as well. Sure enough, I got the job. Although after half a summer there, minus the facade, I didn't get an offer. C'est la vie.

Had my classmate felt she'd done a good deed or thought about me afterward? I don't know. There was something narcissistic in her analysis. But for all that this is so, I still appreciated her words. Was I looking for crumbs off the table? Someone on the "other side of the desk" like her (in essence) to at least notice me? This she did, and I couldn't help but be grateful.

But again that was a weak moment in time for me. And even now when I am feeling so much stronger, I can't deny Sharon's pain or gratitude of that moment, however sad or misplaced it was. Perhaps we do want something even more than true equality. Something like kinship.

Audre Lorde, award winning poet, author and activist, wrote the following passage in a letter to Mary Daly, a lyrically powerful writer and a self-described white, lesbian, radical, feminist author of Gyn/Ecology. After four months of no reply from Daly, Lorde then published the writing as an open letter to a community of women:

Mary, I ask that you re-remember what is dark and ancient and divine within yourself that aids your speaking. As outsiders, we need each other for support and connection and all the other necessities of living on the borders. But in order to come together we much recognize each other. Yet, I feel that since you have so completely unrecognized me, perhaps I have been in error concerning you and no longer recognize you.

She continues:

The oppression of women knows no ethnic or racial boundaries true, but that does not mean it is identical within those differences. Nor do the reservoirs of our ancient power know these boundaries. To deal with one without even alluding to the other is to distort our commonality as well as our differences. For beyond sisterhood there is racism.

I hope that many heard Audre's powerful call to unity and affinity. I agree that we should all be in each other's consciousness. I stand by this belief. Hope?

Belonging

I am at a meeting of the Women of Stanford Law. I've been invited to come and participate and talk about why more women of color, like myself, are not involved.

I attend the meeting and discover somewhat to my surprise that I care what my answer is. My being there is more than just a favor to a friend. It means something to me personally.

Why aren't there more women of color involved in WSL?

When we arrive at SLS we are de facto members of two organizations: BLSA and WSL (or whatever other minority group one is a member of—SLSA, NALSA, or AALSA as the case may be). That's not even including whatever special interest groups one might like to join. For me it was the Entertainment Law Society and the *Stanford Law Journal* during my first year. During second year it was *Stanford Law Review*, the East Palo Alto Community Law Project and the Multicultural Council, the group several of us started to bring together different races, cultures, genders and sexual orientations.

How do we balance all this? We usually end up forced to choose between our womaness or our blackness. Even within these individual organizations there seems no room for special understanding for the choice we've made. Most of the time, we don't realize it ourselves.

But I've grown to realize the value and power of my womaness and blackness. As well as my need to belong to both groups, because they encompass me. Or almost.

So then it came time to run for co-chair of BLSA or WSL; I chose to run for WSL, although I promised myself I would continue to be active in BLSA as well, which I was.

Caterpillar to Butterfly

Finally though, I came into my womanhood. I learned more about feminism and how I connected to it and how I differed. I felt a sense of unity in our identity as women, with other women of varied colors and backgrounds that I'd never really thought about before—always in the past thinking of us as people and friends, but not focusing upon our unique power as women.

I uncovered sexism in myself, in my friends and in my relationship with Matthew, and it shocked me. I realized it had been there but I'd unquestioningly accepted it. It is so much more difficult to identify and then question a problem than it is to simply live with it in ignorance. Who was it who said, "Ignorance is bliss"?

I applied to and was accepted into the first SLS class offered on gay and lesbian rights, sexual orientation and the law, taught by an awesome lawyer from San Francisco. We had the opportunity to focus in-depth on the law's treatment over the years of gays and lesbians as individuals and in relationships.

We established the first Women's Week at SLS and hoped that for a week the school would celebrate, think about, question and challenge itself on women's issues. It was a success.

Still my feelings were angry and confused. Was my life, my consciousness, all coming together or falling apart?

I began to do work with an incarcerated mothers organization. I researched and wrote about incarcerated mothers for my law review note. Mostly these women are young, poor and women of color. I empathize, yet I am at SLS.

I attended the first Women of Color in the Law Conference at Yale Law School. Finally I saw, gathered in one place, women of color whose experiences echoed my own here at Stanford. I am overjoyed, rejuvenated, invigorated, reborn. I am whole again. After two years of self-doubt at SLS, the answer lies before me in the beautiful faces of those women who testify, and survive and live.

Like me. Like our sisters of yesterday and tomorrow.

You damn right it's hard. No shit. What else is new?

I guess my mother could have answered the question my first day. But I had to figure it out for myself. Not that the nuances hadn't changed . . . but the underlying issues and challenges often remain the same. I have to come to my own recognition of my intelligence, confidence, hard work, beauty and the struggle that is . . . the black woman. Plain and simple.

Things finally start falling into place. Patricia Williams, black woman law professor, comes to speak at SLS. And it came to me that this system that allows so few Pat Williamses in our midst denies me the knowledge of choice so many others take for granted. I can be a law professor and teach in my own voice.

I read an article written by a black woman law professor, Judy Scales-Trent, on the concept of women of color as a separate and insular minority. Basically, she talks about the fact that the sum total of oppression experienced by women of color is greater and different from that experienced by men of color and that experienced by white women. I found this analysis enlightening and persuasive, at least in the law field arena where sexism and racism are very much present. I appreciated her identifying the uniqueness of the status of women of color in this nation. This by no means diminishes the oppressive pain suffered by men of color or white women. It is, however, important to acknowledge the differences so we can better struggle against all forms of oppression.

As I grow in self-confidence, I develop my own style. I take pride in my "voice," although I recognize simultaneously that to continue to speak in my voice is to pay a price. Many don't understand or try to understand, and as such devalue the words of me and people like me. To write a law school final in my voice is to receive a grade at variance with the white, male, heterosexual voice I've been frankly told by other friends, most often white and occasionally black, to use to achieve a 3.8.

Being Whole

Still, I've reawakened to loving my voice as I did before I arrived at SLS. I even feel it's become more trained and better able to express itself. It's used the instruction of SLS to more finely hone but not alter its timbre.

One of my favorite readings is Audre Lorde's "Use of The Erotic: The Erotic As Power." She struck a chord deep within me when I read:

It is a short step from there to the false belief that only by suppression of the erotic within our lives and consciousness can women be truly strong. But that strength is illusory, for it is fashioned within the context of male models of power.

As women, we have come to distrust the power that rises from our deepest and nonrational knowledge. We have been warned against it all our lives by the male world, which values this depth of feeling enough to keep women around in order to exercise it in the service of men, but which fears this same depth too much to examine the possibilities of it within themselves.

Is it too much to ask to incorporate instinct and feeling with rationality, analysis and legal theory? Why should it be when certainly these factors are present in our psyches no matter how much we may choose to deny it or pretend it doesn't exist.

Is the law some form of Ten Commandments imprinted on stone tablets from God? Or is it person-made and, therefore, should be inclusive of all that is?

Is my way of looking at life too real or exactly the opposite? In a moment of rebellion and exhaustion I wrote this poem:

My head is in the clouds,
My body floating through life
Do I seem a bit off center?
Or more on center than most?

Still, I know I can't just exist up there . . . in the clouds. I don't even wish to. I am searching for a way to combine spirit, soul, mind, body, idealism and realism all in one Sharon.

Sometimes things seem so clear to me and I express them and get labeled

what?

Too real?

Is there such a thing as being too real for academia?

Should there be?

At least I am too real. I am a black woman, and although that often hurts, there is beauty in knowledge and in being and in identifying and living the struggle and the goal.

And in being who I am and living this journey, I am glad that my chosen path has led me to Stanford Law School where I have learned so much, not just about the law in its strengths and weaknesses, but about myself in mine. I wouldn't have it any other way—and I wouldn't rather be at any other law school than here. I know my instincts led me to the right place for this journey.

Problems here at SLS, and in this world, are discussed on so many different levels and planes of thought. Martin Luther King, Jr. talked about the need for empathy. Here's that recurring theme again.

There is the need for some folks to give something up, share the power, so to speak. But they have to want to do this for us all to really get along, which means convincing them, or ultimately fighting them and taking "it" away. What type of society will we have then, if this change occurs through force?

I don't want to be on top over anyone else. I want us all to be happy in our equality. How idealistic can you get?

Alice Walker, in talking about the relationship between a black husband and wife, wrote the following statement. Although she is talking about this couple's relationship, it seems to me that the statement could be equally telling of relationships between oppressors and the oppressed:

He knows that to make love to his wife as she really is, as who she really is—indeed to make love to any other human being as they really are—will require a soul rending look into himself.

September 1, 1988 • God, it's been too long since last I wrote.

I thought this book was lost to me forever. I am so happy that it is back. One of the maintenance men found it in front of our building and put it in a big black trash bag; and there it sat in the maintenance room one step away from the incinerator. In all these months, thank God it didn't get burned up as trash. One day when Mommy was rushing in after a hectic day of work from her new job as an assistant principal, this maintenance man asked her if she had a daughter named Sharon Simpson, and he gave her the bag! There was everything safe and sound. (Well, except the suitcase was gone.) But that's OK, my journal is back.

September 2, 1988 • In honor of my journal being back, I've written a new poem to welcome it home.

TILT-A-WHIRL
If you asked me today
How to hold on and not
Fall off the tilt-a-whirl
I'd tell you to learn to brace your feet.
But while you're figuring that out
You'd better be standing tall.
And holding on tight.
Leaning into the ride

And not so much anticipating the next turn
As knowing you've got
A damn good grip

September 3, 1988 • Once again, here I am on a plane. Relieved to be in my favorite aisle seat. Even after all these years, I still hate the window.

And even though there is a stranger in the seat beside me instead of my family, I picture me, Sherry, Mommy and Daddy flying to Europe on that long-ago trip, and it still makes me smile.

My journal's on my lap. The feeling of it so familiar in my hands. As I lightly grip the pen, my thoughts spilling out onto the page as fast as I can write, I am again struck by the joy and freedom of thoughts transformed into words on my pages.

Where am I headed for this time? Puerto Rico.

Third year of law school, and so much road has been traveled, I figure it's time to shake it up and get moving on the next chapter of my life. So here I am on my way to work at La Comision Para Los Asuntos De La Mujer, Oficina del Gobierno (or the Commision for Women's Affairs, Office of the Governor). This is work I believe in; la Comision works to lead Puerto Rico in the struggle against domestic violence, sexual harassment and violence against women. It's my externship, and I'll be there until Christmas. My heart led me to find work with a Latina women's organization outside the continental U.S., and I've found the perfect place! People said it would be hard to find, but anything worth doing is worth searching for. I'll be working with women, my sisters from all life experiences, and honing my Spanish and doing work I love.

I'll miss Matthew, Lena, Krista, Catherine, Gina and all my friends—really, school itself—but I *know* this is what I am supposed to do next. The known. And I'm headed for the unknown.

I've got to listen to my heart and follow where it leads me. And even though, OK, yes, I'm a bit scared, I'm excited and ready, too.

I stop and check to make sure I've got Me, Sharon, securely strapped in for the ride. Yes, I'm here. In mind, body, spirit and soul. Of course, I'm sure the ride is going to get hectic. I don't know what is going to happen next.

Just the way I've grown to love it.

RAW POEM

To write or talk or think
Or be
Or not to be
Me
Trying to ignore the
"you talk white"
And I'm thinking
If I talk white, what's my poetry?
And yet, it is me
So what else can I write?
I'm thinking I don't talk white
I talk like me
I am black, African American, yellow, brown, light, coffee,
caramel, dark, tan, gold
Whatever you want to call it
My hair is long, short, fake, real, curly, thick, thin, straight, kinky,
whatever you see it as.
I am fat, skinny, old, young, pretty, okay, beautiful, eh.
It's all in the eyes of . . .
I am black and loud and down or corny, quiet or crazy, white-sounding
or niggerish, high class, aloof, snotty, or wild.
I can't keep up.
I'm holy or heathen, sinner or saint.

So I might as well be the me I know
Because otherwise I could go crazy trying to conceive of and understand
everyone else I am allegedly supposed to be.
Yeah.

I'm sweet or nasty
Self-centered or a sucker
I'm savvy, shy, I'm straight or full of subterfuge.
I'm tired. I'm wired. I'm. I'm. I'm.
I'm a writer and I know it.
I write poetry.
I dig into the deepest parts of myself
Wrestle with my most buried, confounded emotions
Drag them to the surface
Let them gulp in huge breaths of air
Then I gently massage, pull, tuck, soothe, stroke
Until they tell their story
And are at last
At peace.

Pack Your Voice

DON'T LEAVE HOME WITHOUT HER. DON'T LOSE her along the way. No matter how hard you have to swim against, or with, the tide, pack yourself, your Voice . . . your song.

My Voice got lost for a while, even silenced at times, but never gone. Through the course of my travels, I alternately found, lost, rediscovered, nurtured, feared, mistrusted and ultimately came to celebrate my Voice. And now I recognize that all of these stages on my journey are the very means by which I grow and progress.

Throughout the journey shared here, and beyond to new challenges, questions and discoveries . . . graduation from Stanford Law School, the work of social change, astonishing love and extraordinary lessons and loss, my Voice is with me . . . singing my life's song.

There's this wonderful saying, written on a card that many women friends give each other in love and encouragement and celebration.

"I came to live out loud!"

Claiming one's Voice with ultimate rejoicing.

Lena gave me the card recently, and it hangs on the wall near my desk.

Yesterday I found my Voice. Today I'm here to shout about it.

The journey ahead . . .

Pack Wings

At twenty, I'll learn the art of the irrevocable
At thirty, I'll learn to love myself
At forty, I'll fly a plane
At fifty, I'll create an industry
At sixty, I'll claim knowledge,
beyond simply for knowledge sake
At seventy, I'll invent a startling technology
that will have them standing in line
At eighty, I'll discover new and immeasurable ways
of showering joy
At ninety, I'll learn Italian
At one hundred, I'll fly as a newborn baby.

Go forth sweet spirit
Fulfill my destiny

Acknowledgements

Thank you to God, the Creator for infinite love, grace and joy, for giving me this book's vision and the strength and faith to share it, and for the eternal blessings of this passage:

Philippians 4: 8-11
whatsoever things are true, whatsoever things are honest, whatsoever things are just, whatsoever things are pure, whatsoever things are lovely, whatsoever things are of good report; if there be any virtue and if there be any praise, think on these things . . . and the God of peace shall be with you always.

This loving message is long, so please bear with me . . .
Thank you with all my heart and soul to:

My beloved husband and soulmate, Dr. Robert L. Joseph for your love and passionate vision from the very beginning and before; for belief, faith, and for being the most amazing man and spirit, and to his company extraordinaire . . . VizMotion, Inc. for its tireless support and contribution

My mother, my She-ro Beverly

My beautiful sister and twin kindred spirit through the ages, Sherry

Her wonderful husband, my brother Dave, and extraordinary niece and nephew Aria and Maxwell

My father, my friend John

My angelic touchstone, eternal reviewer, and inside my brain partner, Therese

My Soars coach, perennial blossom, no matter what the circumstance soul of generosity reviewer and gentle warriorsister, Brenda

My dream weaver partner, reviewer, stand for Soars and little soaring spirits, Kiwi . . . creator of beauty and joy with Kiwi Kollectibles, Inc.

My sister-in-law and true sisterfriend Jacquelyn for tireless work, research, commitment and belief

Insightful, lovingly honest reviewers traveling the journey - who bore with me every draft of the way: Beatrice, Debra, Jacque and Robin

My new mother and daddy for your beautiful love together and the love you give me

For our love, joys, tears and laughter always: Cheryl, Kevin and my NY Family

Millie, for love at first sight, holding each other up, jumping in harm's way and a great glass of chardonnay

The spiritual journey, discovery, miracles, prayers, blessings and sisterhood of PJ, Jen, Andrea, Suzie, Patrice, Olga and the Los Angeles Women's Bible Circle Sisters, the Atlanta Circle of Grace Sisters and to my church homes God, Self and Neighbor Ministries and West Angeles, Church of God In Christ

My darling sisterfriends - running buddies, we keep each other joyful, sane and healthy: Donna, Lisa and Debra and fitness trainer and friend, Linda

Fi, for your I Corinthians 13 spirit, sharing Soars with so many and your friendship

All those I call family, my dear communities:

Sylvia, Laura, Nancy and the La Jolla Family, Nancy, Andy, and the Bay Area Family, my Los Angeles Family, Atlanta Family, Stanford Family, Pensacola, FL Family, Paterson, NJ Family, Mom Dean and my Queens Family, Boulder, CO Family, the Magnificent Seven, our Spirit Soars Bookclub and the Landmark Crew

Anna, for your early belief in my writing

Sydney and Avater, for your invaluable hard work in the early days

Rose Matsui Ochi, for your gracious mentoring

All my precious relatives and ancestors on Mommy's and Daddy's sides

Homewood Suites of Boulder, CO and San Jose, CA for truly being a home away from home

And of course, my dear cocker spaniel Henry for all your unconditional love and licks

To my own soulspirit for the everlasting journey

To all those who travel this journey with me, touch and enrich my life and allow me to be student, teacher, and fellow sojourner

And the angels that watch over us all.

The Amazing Professionals of this Creative Business:

Association of American Publishers and Publishers Association of the South for expertise and friendship and for welcoming Spirit Soars into the fold so seamlessly

E. Andrew Norwood, attorney-at-law and great person

Drollene P. Brown, phenomenal editor and woman, who always packs power and illumination

Jill Mason, magnificent editor who even early on, really got it!

Monica Stewart, brilliant artist and newfound friend, whose painting Rejoice encouraged my spirit to soar long before Rejoice graced this book's cover

Jill Dible, sensational graphic artist of layout and design who captured the essence of this journey for all to share

J. Stanford Fisher, proofreader of outstanding skill and heartfelt conversation

Nancy Hanger and Andrew Phillips of Windhaven Press, exceptional proofreaders and generous advisers, for bringing Soars all the way home!

WIND BENEATH SOARS' WINGS SPONSORS

Thank you for your friendship, your generosity and profound contribution:

Elizabeth Echols
Millie Escobedo
Kathy Jackson
Leesa Kellum
Marc and Johnelle Roberts
Brenda Romney
Therese Salmon
Robert White